GOOD DEBT,
BAD DEBT

PORTFOLIO

GOOD TO GREAT
BAD

Jon Hanson

GOOD DEBT, BAD DEBT

*Knowing the Difference
Can Save
Your Financial
Life*

Portfolio

PORTFOLIO
Published by the Penguin Group
Penguin Group (USA) Inc., 375 Hudson Street, New York, New York 10014, U.S.A.
Penguin Group (Canada), 10 Alcorn Avenue, Toronto, Ontario, Canada M4V 3B2
(a division of Pearson Penguin Canada Inc.)
Penguin Books Ltd, 80 Strand, London WC2R 0RL, England
Penguin Ireland, 25 St. Stephen's Green, Dublin 2, Ireland
(a division of Penguin Books Ltd)
Penguin Books Australia Ltd, 250 Camberwell Road, Camberwell, Victoria 3124, Australia
(a division of Pearson Australia Group Pty Ltd)
Penguin Books India Pvt Ltd, 11 Community Centre, Panchsheel Park,
New Delhi–110 017, India
Penguin Group (NZ), Cnr Airborne and Rosedale Roads,
Albany, Auckland 1310, New Zealand (a division of Pearson New Zealand Ltd)
Penguin Books (South Africa) (Pty) Ltd, 24 Sturdee Avenue,
Rosebank, Johannesburg 2196, South Africa

Penguin Books Ltd, Registered Offices: 80 Strand, London WC2R 0RL, England

First published in 2005 by Portfolio, a member of Penguin Group (USA) Inc.
1 3 5 7 9 10 8 6 4 2

"The Six Simple Principles of Viral Marketing" from *Demystifying Viral Marketing*
by Dr. Ralph Wilson. Used by permission of the author.

Publisher's Note
This publication is designed to provide accurate and authoritative information in regard to the
subject matter covered. It is sold with the understanding that the publisher is not engaged in
rendering legal, accounting, or other professional services. If you require legal advice or other
expert assistance, you should seek the services of a competent professional.

LIBRARY OF CONGRESS CATALOGING-IN-PUBLICATION DATA
Hanson, Jon.
Good debt, bad debt : knowing the difference can save your financial life / Jon Hanson.
p. cm.
Includes bibliographical references and index.
ISBN 1-59184-073-2
1. Finance, Personal. 2. Consumer credit. 3. Debt. I. Title.
HG179.H265 2005
332.024′02—dc22 2004053400

This book is printed on acid-free paper. ∞

Printed in the United States of America
Set in Adobe Garamond Designed by Francesca Belanger
Illustrations by Patty Kadel

To Nita, Aubrey (A. C.), and Paige—my wife, son, and daughter. Lord Bacon wrote, "He that hath a wife and children hath given hostages to fortune; for they are impediments to great enterprises, either of virtue or mischief." I say Lord Bacon was wrong; I have found a quite opposite truth. My family is the reason behind all I do. It is the reason for this book. It is true that many use their responsibilities as an excuse rather than motivation. A loving family causes a dynamic motivation that far exceeds the static "cost" of family. A loving family should be a mandate to strive for greatness. My family is.

Preface

A Near-Debt Experience

It was summer 1997. I awoke lying on a hospital gurney. In the background I could hear the *beep, beep, beeeep* of a heart monitor—*my* heart monitor. I panicked. This is how it ends? Am I going to die in debt, cowering from the IRS? What will my family think? What have I been doing wrong?

I closed my eyes and hoped that it was all a bad dream. But then I remembered: I had been feeling pressure in my chest for a few days. My wife had finally persuaded me to go to the emergency room.

Still, I was fairly certain that any pain I felt was from my present financial predicament and *not* a heart attack. As I lay there alone in the ER, I realized I was cold. I was wearing one of those fashionable hospital gowns that open in the back, and I had a sheet stretched over me up to my neck: a white one, just the type a nurse would pull up over my head before telling my wife that *debt had killed her husband.*

> *"He showed great promise early in life. Unfortunately, he expired before much could be made of it."*

I imagined that the obituary would say, "Jon Hanson (41) of Pickerington, Ohio, died Tuesday from complications stemming from lack of discipline, inability to delay gratification, and lack of discernment in financial matters. He showed great promise early in life. Unfortunately, he expired before much could be made of it."

Tell Me Where It Hurts

Dr. Gentile (his real name) walked in. He was a cheery sort. The kind of guy you really hate when you are in the middle of feeling sorry for yourself.

"We're having chest pains, Mr. Hanson?" said the doc.

"I don't know about you, but I am," I half replied, half growled.

As he scribbled something on his clipboard, I imagined that he was checking off a box next to "Sarcasm gland good." He had the look of a competent professional ready to dig for answers until he discovered my ailment or my insurance coverage ran out.

We went through family history and the usual questions. Based on the answers, Doc Gentile decided to admit me to the hospital.

"We don't know if you have had a heart attack," he said, "but with your age and family history, you are a prime candidate."

"Doc," I argued, "I really think the pain in my chest is just stress."

"It might be."

"But Doc, I owe the IRS $78,987.54!! *That's* my problem!"

"No, Mr. Hanson," Dr. Gentile calmly replied. "Your chest pains can't be from the IRS. The IRS is a stabbing, rectal pain."

I tried to laugh, and maybe I did, but it wasn't a deep laugh because I really did owe a small fortune to the IRS.

After a battery of tests, I was released late the next day. I found little comfort in being right about the source of my pain. My chest pains were diagnosed as musculoskeletal stress.

Back to Work

Actually, aside from IRS problems, I was in pretty good shape. But as far as mental comfort goes, it was like having one foot in ice water and the other in boiling oil. Then, a year or so later, I received an offer on a rental property, sold it, borrowed some more money, and paid off the IRS in full. I was exhausted from the past seven years of the "poor me" litany that had been running nonstop through my head: "It's not fair. It's just not fair. How could they do this to me? I only owed $26,000!"

There's an upside. Seven years in tax purgatory taught me a thing or two. Be they fair or not, I must deal with my problems head-on as they arise. Fair has little to do with reality. I spent $5,000 in attorney and accounting fees to stretch out the problem while looking for a way out. The result? It cost me about 30 percent more to resist. All of the books on negotiating with the IRS and paying your taxes off for pennies on the dollar are great—if you don't have any assets. After seven long years, I finally admitted my stupidity and accepted the consequences I could not avoid.

After I paid the IRS, I began thinking about the internal dialog I'd had with myself in the hospital. I knew that I needed a change. With past mistakes fresh in mind, I decided to write the book I myself needed to read! Over the next four years, my research took me on an unprecedented trip through my past, my beliefs, and my poor habits. I reasoned that if success leaves clues, so should failure.

> *The harder I looked for something to blame for my failure, the more often my own fingerprints showed up.*

The harder I looked for something to blame for my failure, the more often my own fingerprints showed up. Most clues led to my lack of the three Ds: discipline, deferral, and discernment.

Back to the Books

Almost everything good that has happened to me came from lessons I read in a book. Certain books can confirm your path or inspire change. Books were my way out of a life of poverty. Books helped replace, repair, and improve the areas of my life where parents or teachers were not available to me. Writing is my way to help others escape or improve their lot in life. And so it is natural that I want to leave, as my legacy, a book for those I love. Many ideas I share in *Good Debt, Bad Debt* flow from my journals dating back almost thirty years. Those willing to look closely will find that financial success or failure lies in the ordinary affairs of daily life.

A few months after the September 11 terrorist attacks, I was back in the hospital for a hernia surgery and feeling rather mortal, so I decided to write a more exhaustive journal than I had been keeping. This was to be left as a guideline for my family to follow should I prematurely assume room temperature. The night before the surgery, in a rather disturbing rush of clarity, I asked myself a simple question: If I were going to die tonight, what *should I have* taught my son and daughter about life, relationships, and money? My answer became the outline for *Good Debt, Bad Debt.*

One afternoon in late 2002, I was at a local Bob Evans Restaurant editing my superjournal. I had about twenty-eight pages of a rough draft spread out on the counter. One page shouted, in its forty-eight–point boldface heading, "A Matter of Life and Debt!" A waitress, whom I now think of as Tamara the Waitress, asked if she could take a look. She read a few pages and said, "This is great! Can I take it with me?"

She seemed so enthusiastic that I decided, Why not? Over the next few weeks, whenever I would ask for my pages back, she would say, "My roommate is reading them," "My sister is reading them," "I want my dad to see them," or, finally, "I made some copies for friends. Is that OK?" This went on for a month or more and then I never saw her again. So, while my family is the reason I began to write *Good Debt, Bad Debt,* it was actually Tamara the Waitress who started me thinking that maybe I had something that other people would want to read. Thanks, Tamara, wherever you are.

Making the Rest the Best

Over the years, I have met many people who felt trapped by debt or circumstances. In short, their lives have ceased to be fun. Dragging the dead horse of debt is tiring; it is difficult to move forward while you are always paying back.

Both times that I made major career adjustments I was in very low debt mode. The first was in 1981, when I left a large grocery chain called Kroger's to start a real estate business, and the second came only recently, when I closed my real estate business to write and speak full-time. In 1981, my only desire was money, and real estate seemed to promise that. Twenty-four years later, I am still fond of money. But it is not number one on my list. Time for family and friends and a career that I am passionate about are higher priorities. I want to make the rest of my life the best of my life.

> *Dragging the dead horse of debt is tiring; it is difficult to move forward while you are always paying back.*

As I start the second half of my life, whether I make more or less money matters little to me. I want to follow God's plan for me. I don't want to die leaving books unwritten, poems unspoken, loved ones unloved, and lives around me unchanged.

To position myself as being anti–consumer-debt is not something I take lightly. It may be fun to proclaim catchy lines like "From the guttermost to the uttermost, debt affects us all." But the awful truth is, it really does.

My passion is sharing the message of *Good Debt, Bad Debt,* whose most basic lesson is "The past is the past, unless you still owe for it." This message, for me, is absolutely foundational.

Acknowledgments

Foremost in my memory are my real father and mother, who both died young after a hard life, but always encouraged me to press onward. Of course, I thank my wife, Nita, and her parents for taking me into their family and loving me, even though I am not always lovable. It would be impossible to acknowledge all the other people who have influenced my life, but here are a few:

- My posthumous mentor Dr. Orison Swett Marden. Dr. Marden died in 1924, having written at least seventy books beginning at age forty-six in 1894. I have benefited from his legacy.
- My four adopted fathers: Aubrey C. (Buck) Bennett, Robert L. Teague Jr., Jack Miller, and Jimmy Napier. Taking the best from all of them has been invaluable.
- Indispensable friends for more than twenty years, advisers, encouragers, and early readers: Dave Bennett, Dan and Tracy Haubeil, Thomas G. Ruprecht, James B. Wootton, and Barney Zick.
- Tom Hopkins, who in 1981 pulled me on stage "to do the thing I feared most! Speak!" Tom taught me to always fail forward. Those five minutes changed my life.
- Jim Rohn, Dr. Denis Waitley, and Brian Tracy, though I know them only through books and audio recordings. All have provided valuable counsel and inspiration.
- Seth Godin, whom I only know by reading his books. He

taught me to think outside the box. In fact, he taught me to ask if we even need a box.

- Mark Victor Hansen, my book-marketing mentor. My son Aubrey (A. C.) and I appreciate all he has done for us.

- The entire team at Portfolio: Adrian Zackheim, Megan Casey, Will Weisser, Stephanie Land, Allison Sweet, Jennifer Paré, and others I may not have met. I am thankful they took a chance on a new writer.

Contents

Conclusion   234

Illustrations

Introduction:
A Matter of Life and Debt

Never itch for anything you aren't ready to scratch for.
—Ivern Ball

It is hard to fit yourself for joy while spending money on temporary happiness.
—Jon Hanson

How are you doing?
How are you *really* doing?
Are you financially fit or financially spent?
Are you scratching it up or stacking it up?
Are you living the life you imagined—or an unimaginable life?

In America we have both enjoyed and abused the privileges of our society. Yet many are experiencing an implosion of insecurity and vagueness of purpose that leaves them vulnerable to clever merchants seeking to plunder their infant wealth.

Just what are you working *for?* A quick test: Take your net worth and divide it by the number of years you have worked. What's your result? Seem lower than you thought? This number is how much you are working for per year. The rest is gone, burned up, consumed. It has gone to burn rate, which is described later in this introduction and in Chapter 3. There are other important measures of wealth, such as income, but you'll soon find that income and net worth like to hang out together. If your net worth is $100,000 and you have worked for ten years, you are effectively working for $10,000 a year, even if your actual income is $75,000 a year or more. Don't feel bad. With bad debt, some are working for room and board only; others have a negative net worth.

Certainly life is more than getting and spending money, but because money does necessarily and inescapably affect so many areas of life, it is the main focus of our attention in this book. *Good Debt, Bad Debt* is not about living a starved or pinched existence. It is about gaining perspective and right-sizing spending and saving while keeping retirement aspirations in line. It is about developing a philosophy of debt—or, for many people, a philosophy of no debt. *Good Debt, Bad Debt* encourages us to avoid the consumer entitlement mentality that can only lead to debt, regret, and broken dreams—not to mention a garage and basement full of junk.

What Good Debt *Is*

Good debt increases your net worth. Good debt helps you make money; the use of good debt adds to current earnings, net worth, or foreseeable earning ability. On the other hand, bad debt decreases your net worth. Bad debt takes your money. Payments on bad debt reduce cash flow. Compare:

GOOD DEBT	BAD DEBT
• Earns its keep	• Is typically for consumption
• Increases your net worth or cash flow	• Decreases your net worth or cash flow
• Secures a discount that can be converted to cash or net worth	• Absorbs future earnings
• Creates a leveraged position with a strong margin of safety	• Examples: car loans that rob your retirement fund; continuous credit card debt

- Examples: debt for real estate
  at a safely leveraged level, debt
  for education that can be
  applied for a return of
  capital, debt for a business you
  are competent to operate

What Good Debt *Isn't*

It's easy to rationalize anything we want to do with our money. Advertisers even train us to overcome our own objections! We have all done this; I have done it many times in my life. Whether your excuse is to feel better about yourself or the catch-all "I deserve it," the fact is that rationalizing debt and calling bad good does not change the reality of your financial position. Stacking bad debt on a good asset does not make it a good debt.

Refinancing of personal residences has become a popular sport in America. It can be good, if done for the right reasons. The problem is that many people refinance to pull out cash or lower their payments, only to increase their debt with their new-found cash flow. For many, it only

> *Stacking bad debt on a good asset does not make it a good debt.*

means freeing up their credit cards to be maxed out once again. Then they have all of their old credit card debt on their home and a new stack of debt beside it to contend with. Some believe that all debt on real estate is good debt. That is insane. Some lenders are willing to go 110 percent of value on real estate, so without discipline, disaster lies ahead (for both the lender and the borrower). Unless you have a real change of heart and discipline, *do not* stack credit card and consumer debt on your home equity.

If you are considering consolidation of bad debt that will encumber home equity, please read the white paper *Debt Warfare* first. Get it free at www.gooddebt.com.

Monkey See, Monkey Do?

Some Americans are beginning to question the popular notion (fomented by advertisers and popular culture) that everyone must pursue his or her own inclinations, regardless of the damage to self or society. We are seeing the result of promiscuous spending, easy credit, and, in the end, skinny or nonexistent retirement plans. Too often, debt becomes a weapon that we unwittingly turn against ourselves.

In *The Millionaire Next Door*, Thomas Stanley and William Danko discovered that average self-made millionaires save or invest 15 to 20 percent of their disposable income. In *The Overspent American*, Juliet Schor found that average Americans spend 18 percent of their disposable income on consumer debt payments while saving little or nothing. In this sad juxtaposition lies a key premise of *Good Debt, Bad Debt*: "The past is the past—unless of course you still owe for it." Many can't start up the hill of financial freedom because they are carrying a backpack full of debt.

> *We are seeing the result of promiscuous spending. . . . Too often, debt becomes a weapon that we unwittingly turn against ourselves.*

This would be obvious if only we could step back for a moment and look at how we allocate our income. Madison Avenue and the merchants of debt heap the polite fiction "you can have it all" and "you deserve it" upon the average consumer thousands of times each day. The goal of Madison Avenue is to distract you while the merchants of debt pick your pockets.

In a recent radio broadcast Alistair Begg said, "Our society thrives on materialism, cashing in on the sin of covetousness. Its modus operandi is to create within our hearts a longing for the things we do not have. Not only a longing, but also an attitude of need and entitlement. We need it. We deserve it. Especially if someone else has it." Of course, we have free will (to a certain extent). It is up to us how we respond to messages from Madison Avenue.

Fat, Old, and Broke

Isn't it amazing, at least for a time, how resilient our bodies and our finances are? Eventually, though, poor eating and poor financial habits begin to take their toll. In the book *Good Fat, Bad Fat*, Drs. William Castelli and Glen Griffin counseled readers to distinguish between types of fat that clog the arteries and those that are not harmful. In *Good Debt, Bad Debt*, I counsel readers to engage in similar discernment as to consumer debt. The statistics on obesity are eerily similar to the statistics on debt problems. The Employee Benefit Research Institute and the American Savings Education Council report that 66 percent of Americans are unable to save enough for retirement because of current financial responsibilities (debt). Peter Jennings, in a special report on *ABC News*, said that 66 percent of us are overweight. Let's hope the two groups aren't the same people. Being fat is bad enough. Being fat, old, and broke is even worse.

The buildup of cholesterol in our veins is barely noticeable until the restricted blood flow begins to cause problems. Many people go for years with cholesterol-clogged veins, never realizing the problem until it is too late. For some, a stroke or heart attack may be the first warning. For others, death is the first warning.

A similar process operates in our finances. So long as we have enough blood flow, er, cash flow to pay the bills, we don't see a problem. But in the background, too much debt, like too much cholesterol, looms as the number one killer of wealth and possibility. Once we begin to clog our financial arteries with bad debt, we may experience *shortness of opportunities* and *high debt pressure*. Unchecked, this may lead to financial death or at the least a financial infarction.

Debtabetes

In *The South Beach Diet*, Dr. Arthur Agatston writes of becoming healthy and fit through eating the right foods and balancing good carbs and bad carbs together with good fats and bad fats. In *Good Debt, Bad Debt*, I am advocating financial health and fitness through balance of good debt and bad debt. Agatston speaks of "a silent, so-called metabolic syndrome (prediabetes) found in close to half of all Americans who suffer heart attacks." I sense a similar development in many Americans' finances, perhaps a financial prediabetes syndrome. Let's call it pre-Debtabetes. Debtabetes is the inability of the body to break down and eliminate debt because of insufficient cash flow. Debtabetes is most common in the debt-obese and is closely linked to financial strokes—either fatal or temporarily debilitating. To carry the analogy a little further, we could consider spending as your glycemic (blood sugar) index and cash flow as your financial insulin. To be physically fit and financially fit requires awareness and implementation of many similar skills.

Debt Philosophy

Mr. Jim Rohn asks a great question of his audiences: "If we took your philosophy of life, and got it all down on paper, would you be excited about traveling all over the world giving talks on it?" If not, he suggests, you start there—reworking your philosophy. I labored over Mr. Rohn's challenge for months. In fact, it was the driving force behind completing this book. I ultimately wanted a book I could hand to my children and say, "Here are my core financial beliefs—they are as fundamental and as sure as gravity."

Many financial books present supplemental, not fundamental, principles. Financial failure begins in the thinking process before the actual spending. George Orwell said, "People can't write clearly because they can't think clearly." I try to avoid tortured logic and incomprehensible phrases that are the result of a confused mind. I'd expand this to finances too. **Confused thinking causes confused spending.**

After my IRS debacle, as discussed in the Preface, I realized that my primary downfall in the area of finances had been lack of discipline. While I had done pretty well overall, I felt I could have done much better. Here are three traits of my philosophy that apply to finances. To the right of them, you see the parallel yet antithetical traits advertisers and the merchants of debt want you to embrace:

ECONOWISE TRAITS:
1. Discipline
2. Deferral
3. Discernment
Result: *Lasting* **joy**

CONSUMERATI TRAITS:
1. Indifference
2. Immediacy
3. Ignorance
Result: *Temporary* **happiness**

Consumerati versus Econowise

The Consumerati are what I call those who are spendthrifts, living hand to mouth and in general never thinking of tomorrow. Consumerati are proficient at consuming at any cost. For the most part, they are well-meaning people whose ambitions far exceed their obedience to the fundamentals of money. They respond to emotional marketing appeals and, once they run out of cash, it seems only natural to use bad debt or consumer debt to pay for their wants. We all have a little Consumerati in us. According to Cardweb.com, 50 percent of Americans pay the minimum or far less than the balance due on their credit card bill. Twenty-nine percent pay off their cards monthly. Twenty-one percent of all households in America do not have credit cards. The Consumerati are likely to confuse income with wealth. They don't understand an age-old fact that spending, and not income, determines wealth. Income is like a moving river—wealth is like a lake or reservoir. See the beginning of Chapter 3 for more on this.

> *Most men and women do not make their daily decisions based on a calm weighing of risks and benefits.*

The Econowise, on the other hand, think about how today's actions will affect their future. If we merge economy and wisdom together, we come up with the Econowise—people seeking both economy and wisdom. The Econowise plan on paper and understand how burn rate, delayed gratification (Chapter 4), and avoiding the debt effects (Chapter 1) all can work together to create a prudent lifestyle. The sooner you eliminate the waste, lower your burn rate, and begin an Econowise program, the better.

The definition of burn rate is all the money spent that does not increase your wealth. Burn rate is what is consumed and gone forever. Taxes are a major part of your burn rate, together with food, shelter, and transportation.

Give Me the Best

The last five chapters of this book are more about doing than just philosophy building. *Money Magazine* writes that recent studies by economists from New York University have found that a willingness to plan is closely linked to wealth accumulation. Before you dismiss this statement as self-evident pabulum, ask a few acquaintances how to become wealthy. Many will answer, "a large income and an inheritance." A large income is not necessarily a guarantee of wealth. Nor is an inheritance a guarantee of wealth. It can soon be frittered away. On the other hand, income of almost any size when strained through well-trained habits can create wealth.

Both Plans Are Scalable

The planning and saving habits of the Econowise scale to make them wealthy as their income increases over the years. The non-planning and debt abuse habits of the Consumerati likewise scale to make them poorer and deeper in debt as their income increases. In other words, with a Consumerati lifestyle, if you are unhappy with your life while earning $40,000 a year, you will despise it at $110,000 a year.

Life is truly asynchronous. What you do today may not have an immediate effect but may have a very large effect later in life. The whole personal finance field is pretty simple, a near mathematical certainty—until you add in one thing: human emotion. Most men and women do not make their daily decisions based on a calm weighing of risks and benefits. Most are emotional beings who respond to vague if not nonsensical messages such as "You deserve the best." Hold on! Isn't "the best" a plan that will provide you and your family with a lifestyle you've not only dreamed about, but planned for and earned? Don't seek someone else's best—seek a plan you have designed for your life, a plan that is best for you.

It's One Thing to Admit Your Stupidity— It's Another to Escape the Consequences

This is not an offering from the Self-Esteem Is Free Institute. *Good Debt, Bad Debt* is aimed at two distinct groups: those who realize that they are groping in the dark, financially speaking, and those who are doing OK but think they could do a little better. I call the blind gropers the Consumerati. They enable Madison Avenue and the merchants of debt to enjoy record earnings year after year in post-responsibility America.

To Consumerati, delayed gratification is an alien concept. Despite being part of the richest and most educated group in American history, Consumerati suffer deeply from the seeming inability to get a grip on the financial rudder. The Consumerati are, for the most part, slaves to their emotions. They are sure that they must follow their feelings to get what they deserve. The world around them seems to confirm this—they deserve the best, don't they? Consumerati men and women strive to maintain or create an image that is neither healthy nor fiscally responsible. Relax. *Good Debt, Bad Debt* will concentrate on what *you* can do *using your present income.*

My Objectives for *Good Debt, Bad Debt*

Here are my goals for *Good Debt, Bad Debt* as set out in my journal:

1. **Brevity**—To make literary bouillon cubes with a financial flavor.
2. **Wit**—Humor with its thinking cap on. Laugh or smile while learning.
3. **Visual humor**—Cartoons with a lesson of financial frugality.
4. **Incontrovertible arguments**—Arguments with results that are verifiable (knowable) in advance.
5. **Fun**—A book that's fun to write, read, and share; one that creates useful new words and terms.

Brevity. Would you buy a 763-page book called *How to Be Brief*? Mark Victor Hansen of *Chicken Soup for the Soul* fame says that most people have about two hours to spend with a book, perhaps on a short flight from Boston to Atlanta, in the evening at home, or over a couple of lunch breaks. The thinking in the book is no more important than the thinking caused by the book. See www.gooddebt.com for discussion guides.

> *Personal finance is simple, requiring little more than basic math and sincere forethought. We only need add human nature to finance to make it both funny and tragic.*

Wit. My catchphrase for this book is "The past is the past unless, of course, you still owe for it." It seems that many people can't go where they want to go because of where they have been. Truly, what constantly pulls your past into today? Debt. If I tell a church audience, "It's hard to give your heart to Jesus when your butt belongs to Master-Card," they understand the message. Not only is it scriptural, it is common sense. When I refer to spendthrifts and those striving to keep up with their imagined reference group as the Consumerati, and people who follow a plan and seek wisdom as the Econowise, it's easy to follow. It makes sense.

I'd better trade for discipline—I haven't
done too well with just talent.

Visual Humor. Throughout *Good Debt, Bad Debt* you will see original cartoons by Patty Kadel. When I developed an idea for a cartoon, I would put it in writing via e-mail or letter to Patty, who would turn my concept into a drawing. You will probably have your favorite. Here's mine—a guy dripping with talent who suffers from the inability to gain financial traction because he lacks discipline. Talent is only one part of success. If you flip to Chapter 10 ("You Married Who?"), you will see a cartoon on "relationship baggage" that generates a great deal of comment. We have all seen this type of relationship. It's a simple concept, but many overlook it or seemed surprised when the "unpacking" starts. I had a great deal of fun doing the chapter on marriage, an area in which I've done well. My wife, Nita; my son, A. C.; and my daughter, Paige, are a perpetual blessing.

Incontrovertible Arguments. Our arguments must have both texture and depth, or our success will be short lived. After the smile wears off the words, does a residue of wisdom remain? Few will argue with the saying "You must spend less than you make. You must have capital to capitalize." The first five chapters are about developing a philosophy of debt or avoidance of most debt. Except for business or investment debt (at safe loan-to-value ratios), the goal, in time, is to have everything in your personal life debt free.

Fun. Personal finance is simple, requiring little more than basic math and sincere forethought. We only need add human nature to finance to make it both funny and tragic. While fun is not an absolute prerequisite for success, it does make the more mundane but necessary parts of life easier to accept. If you can laugh at others' inability to embrace discipline, delayed gratification, and discernment, then perhaps you can learn these lessons without the unpleasant aspect of firsthand experience.

> *"It's hard to give your heart to Jesus when your butt belongs to MasterCard."*

What's NOT in *Good Debt, Bad Debt*

No quick-fix temporary solutions. No optimistic taffy to soothe your ego. *Good Debt, Bad Debt* is about embracing the reality of where you are at and working to improve your position. You won't find specific to-do lists and forms to fill out. No slavish devotion to budgeting. When your reasons are right and you can foresee the promise of a prudent financial philosophy, you won't need someone to micromanage your life. All things will work together for good for those who embrace sound financial fundamentals. *Good Debt, Bad Debt* will concentrate on what *you* can do *using your present income.*

What's IN *Good Debt, Bad Debt*

How should you think about debt? Is debt good or bad? Can debt be an effective tool? This is a book to help you develop a philosophy of debt, spending, and saving. *Good Debt, Bad Debt* is about fundamentals—time-tested and, sadly, debtor-proven ones. It's about building a foundation for your future.

Some of it is tongue-in-cheek, but not so outlandish that people can't relate to it. For example, in Chapter 1 ("The Debt Effects"), I say, "Credit cards are the crack cocaine of the credit industry." I am not actually accusing the industry of drug pushing, just something close.

Throughout I encourage a healthy skepticism which will allow you to deconstruct advertising and media messages. Think of it this way: you edit what comes into your mind, or else the media and advertisers will. In *Good Debt, Bad Debt* I teach you to question the media and merchant messages you receive hundreds, even thousands, of times a day. When you hear the message "Don't put all of your eggs in one basket," you will wonder if the message was sponsored by the National Basket Makers Association.

Understand the debt effects, manage emotions, deflect media influence, work from a plan, monitor burn rate, delay gratification, track and tabulate expenses, and invest for your future. That's simple enough, right? Grasp the first four chapters and you will have a better understanding of debt and money than 90 percent of Americans. Actually put these fundamentals to work in your life as a financial liturgy, and you will finish financially ahead of 97 percent of Americans. How are you doing? How are you *really* doing?

> *Think of it this way: you edit what comes into your mind, or else the media and advertisers will.*

Chapter One
The Debt Effects:
The Invisible Hand of Debt

The ten-second lesson: "The past is the past—unless, of course, you still owe for it."
　　　　　　　　　　　　　　　　　　　—Jon Hanson

Consumer debt since 1999 has grown an average of 14.6 percent per year.
　　　　　　　　　　　　　　　　　　　—ABC News

Liberty or Debt?

"Give me liberty or give me death!" cried Patrick Henry, admonishing his fellow legislators to take up arms against the British for American sovereignty. That was in 1775. In today's culture of excessive spending, perhaps Henry's cry would be

"Give me liberty or give me debt!" The British have retreated, but millions of Americans, by their own choice, allow credit card companies, mortgage lenders, and every known form of debt or monthly obligation to carry on the work of enslavement. Patrick Henry's famous speech could apply as easily to debt as to death.

It is natural to indulge in illusions of hope—to think that *our* path is unique, that it cannot lead *us* to the same end as it has led others. We hear the siren song of popular culture and we are seduced by it, transforming into the typical consumer. Avoiding responsibility, we are given over to our emotions until finally we collapse under the weight of our own desires.

In America you will not be singled out or made fun of for wasting your resources. In fact, you will have many cheerleaders, although most of the cheerleaders will be people who profit by selling you trinkets and assorted junk. Just because millions of others share this same practice of spending everything they earn does not make it a right or proper path to follow.

The culture of spend, *spend*, SPEND is necessarily created by merchants to keep their coffers overflowing. It has been said that more than 60 percent of the economy is based on consumer spending, in part financed by consumer credit. For those who collect the money, this spending culture is rewarding. For those doing the spending, it is enslaving.

Many speak the language of free men and women, yet daily proceed in the opposite direction.

So What?

The stigma of debt seems nonexistent today. Not so long ago, many Americans regarded debt as a sign that something was morally wrong. Perhaps the availability of credit cards and revolving debt has made us more adventurous and greedy. Also, credit has become abstract and anonymous. Instead of owing the corner grocer and feeling a moral obligation to him, you pay (or don't pay) your credit card bill to a faraway faceless company. The grocer and dry cleaner will still smile and wave hello.

But the "debt effects" linger. Look around—you needn't look far to find someone suffering from the effects of debt. Those not yet suffering may very well be on the road to perdition without even knowing it. Many speak the language of free men and women, yet daily proceed in the opposite direction. Henry Taylor, in *Notes from Life* (1847), wrote, "A right measure and manner in getting, saving, spending, giving, taking, lending, borrowing, and bequeathing would almost argue a perfect man." Today Taylor would change nothing in this sentence other than ending it with "a perfect man or woman."

Not everyone has the moral or intellectual stamina to set into action a purposeful plan for the future. Yet only those who develop a plan and follow it will succeed.

Those who live in a constant state of "want" become slaves to their own passions. Many go further—voluntarily putting on the shackles of debt—not only spending all they earn but also borrowing into their future for today's excesses. When we use debt to acquire products or services, it is not really a payment for the product or service, but a claim on future earnings.

In its early stages, debt causes no pain. On the contrary, the insidiousness of debt lies in the very fact that the use of debt gives its victims temporary pleasure. A large majority of Americans will risk financial leprosy to have the *temporary* pleasure afforded by spending in advance of earning.

Debt—the Equal Opportunity Enabler

Credit to the untrained appetite distorts reality. It provides the emotions with vast avenues to explore. Credit allows emotions to trump math—stretching our purchases far into the future and reducing the "right-now cost" to a few dollars a month. Soon the emotion subsides and you are left with the reality of the math. For some people it's like the directions on a shampoo bottle: apply, lather, rinse, and repeat. Apply credit, lather up your emotions, and rinse away your monthly cash flow. Repeat.

Most consumer credit advertising uses the "bump and pick" method I discuss in Chapter 2 ("Emotional Hostage"). If you have been part of the buy-now/think-later crowd, take a deep breath and think, Now is the time to begin serious change.

Debt Takes More Than Just Your Money

Adam Smith is famous for his theory of the invisible hand of capitalism. He said that laissez-faire (left-alone) markets naturally adjust because of the self-interest of consumers and the owners of capital. I don't dispute the Scotsman's theory. The sentence above is less than a thumbnail sketch of the whole. I bring it up to propose an antithetical theory: the invisible hand of debt. Many of us look fine and probably are as long as we can make the payments for our excesses. But are we really making any financial progress?

> *Credit to the untrained appetite distorts reality.*

What holds us back from financial success? The most evident of my four *debt effects,* loss of cash flow, is easy to see; the others may operate invisibly. In Smith's invisible hand theory, capital seeks opportunity to expand and grow, as it is good for the individual owner of the capital and the consumer. In my invisible hand of debt theory, Consumerati individuals suffer from the invisible or nearly imperceptible loss of both time and opportunity. On one hand, consumer debt (bad debt) fuels capitalist ventures because it creates sales and moves the economy. On the other hand, if too much consumer debt is used, the invisible hand of capitalism metaphorically reaches out to slap the consumer as it morphs into the invisible hand of debt. Once we reach the tipping point with consumer debt (100 percent burn rate), we lose the opportunity to participate in a capitalist society. We are on the road to serfdom.

The Four Debt Effects: The Four Thieves, or How the Invisible Hand Operates

Always remember that debt takes more from you than just money. It is easy to think of debt simply in terms of bills to be paid, but it is so much more. There are four major debt effects:

Loss of freedom
Loss of cash flow
Loss of time
Loss of opportunities

Certainly debt may cause problems beyond these four, but most difficulties come in some form of them.

Loss of Freedom. Debt will eventually keep you from doing what you want to do. When you are loaded with debt, your options narrow considerably. I have often said, "Working while carrying a load of debt is like a prison work-release program. You are released each day to work, but the balance of your time is spent in a mental prison."

Do you work for joy or to avoid the pain of losing your possessions? With a high enough debt-to-income ratio, you may cross a threshold or amount of debt that simply renders earning money a way of avoiding pain. Real progress or joy seems a distant memory.

In ancient Babylon, a slave was able to earn a few extra shekels on his own time, after completing his master's work, to save toward buying his way out of slavery. He could actually redeem (repurchase) himself. We, too, may redeem ourselves from the bondage of bad debt. Perhaps you do not feel like you are in bondage, but if you stop paying your bills, what happens? You find out who your master is. The more bad debt you have stacked up, the more severe your master will be in collecting her due.

Think. When you live and work from week to week, just scratching out a living, are you really any more than an indentured servant? Perhaps you feel like a prisoner who gets weekends off for good behavior. I spent seven years feeling like part of a prison work-release program while I owed a large sum to the IRS. With a high burn rate, are we really any more than a pipeline delivering the fruits of our effort to our creditors?

Is your routine to get up, go to work, come home, eat, sleep, get up, go to work, come home, and eat, only to do it all again the next day? Many people never realize the drudgery of their lives! If we can agree that entry into this cycle is voluntary, then it would follow that leading this lifestyle is also voluntary.

Did you say you are free? Where do you have to be tomorrow? Can you relocate your residence to wherever you want—right now? Or do debts and obligations have a large say in what you do? In Chapter 6 ("What If You Live?"), I discuss wealth metrics; there you find Dr. Buckminster Fuller's simple formula to calculate "useful wealth."

One wit said, "Having a job is like taking a mortgage out on your life." Unless you are born wealthy, you must arrange your escape from drudgery at an early age. Born without wealth, you are at least a part-time servant and are unable to do whatever you want. It is up to you whether you remain in this voluntary servitude or arrange your affairs to carry yourself to financial freedom.

From Success to Significance

Suppose you wish to change careers? If you have a high debt-to-income ratio, debt will certainly be a deciding factor. Following your passion and moving from success to significance careerwise may depend on whether you can downshift from corporate executive at $120,000 a year to teaching children to read at $0 to $30,000 a year. Or perhaps you simply want to take a few years off and write a book. That's what I did, though I had a lot going my way—while my income dropped by over 80 percent, my wife's income increased by over 25 percent. The math does not sound favorable, but our expenses are so low that we have been fine. The interesting thing is that if I had consumer debt, car payments, and high housing expenses, you would never be reading this book. I simply would not have been able to quit my real estate business and take two years to write this book if my expenses or burn rate was large.

Most of us unknowingly choose servitude when we buy into the popular culture of "you can have it all." You can—when you have earned it. Spend the first ten to twenty years of your working career saving and investing 15 to 20 percent of your income rather than choosing to spend 15 to 20 percent of your income to service bad (consumer) debt. If you begin now, you will earn and deserve your freedom.

Freedom, as a concept, is like a hill: often it looks better at a distance. Close up, you begin to see that it can be a lot of work to climb to the top. Freedom means something different to almost everyone. Someone might think that freedom is just having the bills paid. Another person might think that freedom is all the bills paid and $3,000 a month retirement income. And yet another person might think that he or she needs $10,000 a month or more in order to retire. For our purposes, let's just say that financial freedom is a lack of necessary worry or concern about money.

Many people have created fortunes from far less income than you are currently earning, even when adjusted for inflation. When financial difficulties begin, many people believe that they are worse off than anyone who went before them. When you are debt-free, the real freedom is not just what you can do, but what you don't have to do. You are free from the invisible hand of debt.

Loss of Cash Flow. Surely this is the most obvious debt effect. This effect is first noticed when you begin to run out of "walking-around money," a few dollars for incidentals. While most of your disposable income covers the basic necessities, a portion that could be used to eventually replace your job is busy repaying bad debt. While you may not be able to eliminate every bit of consumer debt, it's a pretty safe bet that you can pare it down and begin to invest for your future. If you are spending 15 percent of income on bad debt, the first goal is to get that down to 10 percent, then 5 percent, and eventually nearly zero. Do this while redirecting the cash flow to savings and investments, and eventually this fund alone can replace your job. This won't happen in a short time, but with diligence over ten to twenty years, the results can be amazing. How different would your life be if all the money you spend on consumer debt payments went into savings or an investment? Now consider what that would have meant over the past twenty years or what it will mean over the next twenty years. If you are age forty-something, you may project both ways: to the past and the future.

While you may lament how low the return on savings rates are now (there are other things to invest in), over the years you will realize that returns are not fixed. In 1981 some savings banks were paying 15 percent per annum. The return is not the lesson here, though—the savings habit is the lesson. In the beginning, don't worry about return. Just make sure that you are stacking up the capital. You must have capital to capitalize!

Many sacrifice their true passions to debt. Soon most of their money is allocated to "reparations" or repaying for past spending. Their passions dull into complacency and are soon forgotten. They lose simply by giving debt too large of a vote in their future. Remember, the past is the past, unless of course you still owe for it. It is hard to move forward while paying backward.

Loss of Time. If you're in debt, you must be somewhere other than where you'd like to be. Arnold Bennett, in his 1910 book *How to Live on Twenty-four Hours a Day*, wrote, "The beauty of time is that everyone has the same amount and you cannot spend it in advance." Largely, Mr.

> *They lose simply by giving debt too large of a vote in their future.*

Bennett is correct. But consider people who are deeply in debt—bad debt. They essentially have spent their time in advance, for they are obligated to be at their jobs to repay their debts. They have spent their time in advance of it arriving. This is what I mean by the term *mortgaging your life.* Certainly we sell our skills or brawn in the marketplace, but more than that we must realize that what we sell is part of our remaining time. As you grow in wealth and influence, you will value time more than you do today.

The amount of mental energy expended concerning (worrying) ourselves with bad debt vitiates time we could otherwise spend on positive pursuits. Freedom from debt and time with family and friends have begun to edge out weight loss as the number one New Year's resolution in the past few years. Many people desire free time more than additional money. The wise among us deeply value time for family and friends as well as time to write or perchance to think.

Loss of Opportunities. When you see a great opportunity for financial gain, it is unlikely that you will be able to take advantage of it, because you will be financially unable to do so. The first rule of all enterprise is to know a solid value when you see it. The second rule is to be able to act on an opportunity when it arises. If your neighbor suddenly decides to sell his extra building lot for 50 percent of its true value but only if he can have cash in twenty-four hours, can you respond? This actually happened to me about a year ago (yes, I bought it). The moral of the story is this: *funds already spoken for must remain silent when opportunity knocks.* We lose if we have not developed the habit of preparing for opportunity. It is debilitating to sit and recount lost opportunities, but at the same time they should be lessons that we need not miss the next time. We must embrace the lesson, not the loss; embrace the light, not the dark. Truly this debt effect reaches the heart of all the debt effects. It is the silent killer of possibility and promise. I like to refer to lost opportunities as the ultimate *invisible depreciation.* It's easy to see the effect of depreciation on a new car, an average of $250 or more a month. It's harder to calculate *the benefit* of having that $250 a month accruing in a liquid investment so you'll be ready to seize a tremendous opportunity.

> *Funds already spoken for must remain silent when opportunity knocks.*

For Whom Am I Working?

Many people work hard to have luxuries—only to become slaves to those luxuries. In *The Art of Money Getting*, P. T. Barnum wrote, "Debt robs a man of his self-respect and makes him almost despise himself." You may well ask, Do I have my possessions—or do they have me? After a few years of "prosperity," this is the question I asked myself.

No matter how low a wage you are earning, success is within your reach. Many people refuse to believe this, since they are already living at the financial edge. You probably have everything you need; you may just be using your resources ineffectively.

Some people think that success will start only when they begin to earn a certain dollar amount or when some future event "saves" them. The problem with such thinking is, if you wait to start you may carry forward such poor financial habits that even when—or, more to the point, if—this dollar amount or event happens, it will not be enough to overcome the poor habits you acquired while waiting. The notion "I don't make enough" is more popular than the supremely accurate notion "I have poor spending habits."

For most families or individuals, massive changes aren't needed. Usually just a reallocation of your present income can start you on the path to independence. It is usually your way of thinking and of handling the war of thoughts and desires within you that needs rehabilitation.

A few years ago I wrote in my journal, "Many have a form of wealth but deny its power through lack of discipline and unbridled desire." Your form of wealth is the income you likely have if you are reading this book. Many people never give thought to the right ordering of finances and setting aside a proper portion of their income to offset their advancing age. Your present income can make you wealthy if you are willing to live at 85 to 90 percent of that income during the estate-building years. It is uncomfortable to consider that wealth could have already been acquired from what has long since passed through our hands.

> *"Many have a form of wealth but deny its power through lack of discipline and unbridled desire."*

Hand-to-Mouth

Those choosing to live hand-to-mouth will always be a financially inferior class compared with those who take the time to plan, save, organize, and invest. Some of us compound the problem by choosing to live not only financially hand-to-mouth but also intellectually and spiritually hand-to-mouth, never building a reserve of knowledge and faith for use beyond the immediate moment. To be sure, your intellectual and spiritual development may be nurtured independently of your finances, but the most successful people build all three simultaneously. As an analogy, think of how a cable or rope is made, with three strands of the cable representing your financial, intellectual, and spiritual sides. When all three of these are woven together, they produce a cord that is not easily broken.

In *Thrift*, Samuel Smiles wrote, "Economy is not a natural instinct, but the growth of experience, example, and forethought. It is also the result of education and intelligence. It is only when men become wise and thoughtful that they become frugal. Hence the best way of making men and women provident is to make them wise." If I connect Smiles's recommendation of economy and wisdom together, I come up with what I call the **Econowise**—people seeking both economy and wisdom.

The two main spending styles are Consumerati and Econowise. **Consumerati** spend all the money they have; they are the overspenders. Many Consumerati adopt a consumer entitlement mentality, eventually believing they not only need but also deserve everything they want. The Consumerati avoid the three Ds of discipline, deferral, and discernment while embracing the three Is: indifference, immediacy, and ignorance. I do not mean by *ignorance* that the Consumerati are literally ignorant. I mean that by design they choose to be ignorant in the area of personal finance. Just by being unaware, you are ignorant. It is an ignorance of information, not a lack of intelligence. I am urging you to avoid *willful* ignorance.

The Econowise on the other hand plan for life's demands; they seek economy and wisdom. The question the Econowise ask at the beginning of every spending situation is "Does this take me nearer to or farther from my goals?" A constant training in the Econowise habits is desirable. Make it part of your internal dialog.

The Econowise of course embrace discipline, deferral, and discernment. We could further distinguish between these two types as those who spend all or more than they make (spendthrift/Consumerati) versus those who spend less than they make (thrifty/Econowise). Their cousins are the Insatiable and the Prudent, respectively.

Cultural, social, or economic forces do not create criminals. They are criminals as a result of their own choices. So, too, debtors are created by their own choices just as financially independent people are created by their own choices.

Did You Know?

If you have worked for many years and have little or nothing to show for your efforts, it is because either you don't know the fundamentals of spending or you choose to ignore them. It may be a matter of financial immaturity—or perhaps you have just never been made aware of the fundamentals. Financial immaturity is the major reason that people do not plan for the future. Awareness is the easy part. That's the good news! The ongoing work of leading the life of the Econowise involves awareness of the debt effects, monitoring your burn rate, having a spending plan in place, and having a written plan for an endgame. For the Econowise, the endgame begins when passive income exceeds their needs and they are free to do as they wish. Please, don't misunderstand. I am not against work—just against forced work due to being a slave to one's desires.

Your awareness will control your possibilities. Whatever one person can do, another can do. This sentiment was a staple of Victorian writing. Many of the financial books from that period are full of examples of successes to serve as models. Today most business writers, perhaps reflecting the market, concentrate on quick fixes rather than examples stretching over several years.

Plan, Plan, Plan

It is up to you to plan, study, and seek a wise and prudent life. If you don't know how to become financially competent, you must ask until you do know. What a terrible cost silence imposes on ignorance. A Chinese proverb says, "He who asks a question is a fool for five minutes. He who does not ask is a fool forever."

Awareness can only create a perception of possibilities. You must still muster the maturity to take action. Being full of awareness may make you interesting to talk with—but you could still be a terrible example to follow. You must also choose to be free. The ever-quotable Oscar Wilde said, "It's better to have a permanent income than to be fascinating."

Some people never realize that they can redirect their present incomes and become wealthy. They buy into the popular culture and ignore the wisdom of the ages. You are responsible for your choices. Recast your habits and you will change your life permanently. You may change temporarily by sheer force of will, but it will only be temporary. Habits, in the long run, will control your destiny. Let's examine how education and culture may lead you to make poor choices and how you can avoid them.

It's Your Choice, but "They" Want to Help

For merchants who are armed with psychologists, sociologists, surveys, and ad agencies, the typical consumer is no more than a cow being milked by his or her emotions. When you no longer produce the milk—uh, the payments for your excesses— you are shipped off to the bankruptcy slaughterhouse to have your guts ground into sausage and your hide made into leather bags for ad executives. Then, you are returned to the general population as an empty shell, to start the cycle all over again— unless you learned from the lessons of debt.

Have so many of us really degenerated from freedom seekers to mere cows being milked by our emotions? What do you think?

Many foreigners are amazed to learn that we do not teach saving or investing in our public schools. If we do not learn our financial skills from our parents, where do we learn them? Most people, I suspect, are self-taught—usually after realizing that what they have been doing is not working. Others will never learn.

Surveys show that American children are behind those in many developed countries in math, science, and reading but are number one in the belief that they are the best in the world. Unearned self-esteem is much like consumer credit borrowing—

one day the bill comes due. Wouldn't it be better if Johnny could actually read and do math rather than just *feel* that he can? Won't Johnny's self-esteem be better in the long run if he bases his assumptions on hard facts rather than feelings? Won't Johnny's financial future be better if he understands the full effect of his spending? Shouldn't we teach our children to build a solid financial foundation rather than create an illusion of wealth supported by consumer credit?

Can I Fast-Forward?

Søren Kierkegaard wrote, "Life can only be understood backwards; but it must be lived forwards." Ah, I see the problem. Is it worth all the work to develop an Econowise plan? You can answer that question only by projecting forward and looking back.

Suppose you had a videotape of your future and could fast-forward to see if all the work ahead of you would be worthwhile. Can I give you a hint? If you don't change the way you think and act now, your financial future will look pretty much as it does today. But, if you take steps now, you can change the ending. Remember the thumb-worn creed, "He finished on time, because he started on time." Begin now. Only change now can affect the end of your tape.

Your biggest investment should be in your future. Your future is enriched by applied knowledge of your daily burn rate, retirement, education, reading, and study. A definite purpose, a desire, to have a certain future must be at the center of your plan.

We often fear facing the truth about our careers and ambitions because of the effort it will require to override the debt effects. It's easier to maintain the status quo than to strive for your dreams. Are you able to change your career or follow your dreams? Or are you enslaved to bad debt? Debt makes cowards of us all.

How's Being Broke Working for You?

Sometimes I hear, "That's too much work! Who wants to spend their time planning and thinking, saving, and learning to invest?" Jim Rohn mocks Joe Six-Pack with this line: "Hey, by the time I get home, have a few beers, watch a little TV, I don't have time to study, to learn—to read!" Mr. Rohn incredulously adds, "And he wonders why he is broke?!"

> *Inaction will wear you out!*

Let me ask you this: are you getting any rest being broke? For the most part, being poor is more tiring than treading the path to wealth. And the path to wealth is much less depressing. If you have a mind to improve your lot in life, keep in mind that *inaction will wear you out!*

Good Debt vs. Bad Debt

You can view the differences between good debt and bad debt as much like the differences between good cholesterol and bad cholesterol. Doctors tell us that we need a certain amount of good cholesterol but that too much bad cholesterol will eventually kill us.

We can liken bad cholesterol—LDL (low-density lipoprotein)—to bad debt, which is artery-clogging debt. Good cholesterol—HDL (high-density lipoprotein)—is akin to good debt that clears arteries and keeps you financially healthy. Part of this financial artery-clearing effect is an increase in cash (blood) flow.

I always thought that zero cholesterol was supposed to be my goal. Not so. Apparently if your HDL measurement is under 35, it's a health risk. Your total HDL rating should be 40 or 50, and up to 70 or 80 of HDL can actually protect you against various diseases.

Likewise, some people think that zero debt is best. It sounds good, doesn't it? But zero debt also means zero growth or at the most a low growth rate. Perhaps we can learn from the HDL example. If it takes some HDL to be in good physical health, let's take the mental leap that it takes some good debt to be financially healthy.

The definition of good debt is similar to that of good cholesterol. It keeps the arteries clear. Good debt keeps the cash flow running smoothly and the funds pumping. When you read the definitions below, notice that good debt is a debt on assets that produce a return above their cost. It is debt on assets that create cash flow in excess of the cost of the debt. It is not debt that kills. Remember this: when you use debt to pay for something, it is not a payment in full, but merely a claim on your future time and earnings.

GOOD DEBT	BAD DEBT
• Earns its keep	• Is typically for consumption
• Increases your net worth or cash flow	• Decreases your net worth or cash flow
• Secures a discount that can be converted to cash or net worth	• Examples: Car loans that rob your retirement fund, continuing credit card debt, living on student loans, furniture loans, loans for rapidly depreciating items, loans for parties, weddings, or vacations
• Creates leveraged position ($300 out, $400 in monthly)	
• Examples: debt for real estate at a safely leveraged level, debt for education that can be applied for a return of capital, debt for a business you are competent to operate	

Bad Debt. Bad debt is money owed for trinkets, nonessential essentials, an excess of items, and other consumer junk. For example, a nonessential essential could involve paying $599 a month for a Lexus, without the commensurate cash flow. It is true that you need a car, an essential, but you don't need a car that costs $599 per month. See Chapter 8 ("Driving Your Life Away").

Generally, credit cards, unless paid in full monthly, involve bad debt. Approximately 50 percent of Americans make the minimum payment or don't pay their balances in full each month. Certainly we need clothes, cars, washers, dryers and many other consumer items we sometimes charge. Bad debt usually begins to pile up when we allow emotional spending or spending without regard to consequences. Without a spending plan in place and clear guidelines, we accumulate bad debt quickly.

Plastic Crack

Credit card companies, perhaps taking their cue from drug dealers, send college students sample cards with credit lines of $500 to $2,000 to hook new users (the companies readily admit that they assume the parents will pay). The entry into massive credit card debt is easy. The cards are easy to acquire and often thought to be used for recreational spending. They come to you without prompting—in fact, often with a premium just for signing up. T-shirts and cookies are common premiums on a college campus. **Credit cards are the crack cocaine of the credit industry.** Many victims, after being strung out on credit cards, seek stronger forms of credit when their pusher threatens to cut them off. Some move from credit cards to pawning their home or other assets to feed their credit addiction. While pawning (refinancing) a home can provide temporary relief, many sneak right back to "using" again. Soon they are plagued by "plastic crack" again. Only now the solution of pawning the home is not available.

Credit card companies, perhaps taking their cue from drug dealers, send college students sample cards with credit lines of $500 to $2,000 to hook new users.

The quick high or feeling of power from spending without earning is addictive—it's a difficult habit to break. Some users go through twelve-step programs such as Debtors Anonymous, and others seek help through various debt counseling agencies. Many find themselves completely strung out and dealing with the law. Though going through bankruptcy court is not criminal, it will exact a heavy price to rid you of your demons. The price is financial death and rebirth as a marked man or woman for ten years to life. On many loan applications you must acknowledge whether you have ever filed for bankruptcy—and lying on a loan application *is* criminal. Some lenders will still do business with you, but a large percentage will not. It is a price you pay for being a former credit addict. Thankfully I have been in bankruptcy court only as a creditor trying to collect money. I can tell you this: it is not a happy place. Sadly, many will leave bankruptcy free from debt but not from their addiction to living beyond their income.

Is there such a thing as responsible use of credit cards? Of course. Used responsibly, they can be a valuable and convenient tool. Carrying credit cards is like carrying a concealed weapon. In responsible hands, they benefit the owner; in the hands of the foolish, they are deadly. Coupled with unbridled emotion, credit cards can eviscerate any rational financial plan.

Some of the articles and studies I've seen say that the average student leaves college owing $4,700 in credit card debt and $18,700 in student loans. What is the lesson he has learned? If college only whets young people's appetite for consumer debt and a Consumerati lifestyle, they would be safer not going to college! Don't get me wrong. Go to college; just be careful what you learn.

Bad debt is further defined as spending for debt that reaches into the last 10 to 20 percent of your monthly or weekly income. This statement seems illogical to many people, who say, "I have to spend all I make, because I don't make enough!" For some, this may be true. But for the majority of people reading this book, it is not. I know people who make $150,000 a year and are completely broke, without a dime. I know others who have never made over $15,000 a year and have $150,000 in the bank as well as several prime pieces of real estate. We will explore this further in Chapter 3 ("Burn Rate"). What could you do with all of the bad debt payments you have made over the past ten years?

Paradebt

There is another category I call **paradebt** or "almost debt." This is the cumulative effect of all your nonessential monthly spending. I use the term *paradebt* because, although it's not actually debt, it has a similar effect—the money is gone. Paradebt involves services like cable TV that generally do not involve long-term contracts. They are voluntary monthly obligations that can be canceled at any time. Realize that they are short-term debt. A debt is a debt is a debt.

Death by Debt

When people say, "These bills are killing me!" they may be closer to the truth than they realize. Bad debt can build up deposits in your cash flow arteries, and soon you could have a financial stroke.

At first, the cash flow is only restricted, but sooner or later your reduced cash flow leads to problems. **Shortness of opportunities** and **high debt pressure** are the most common symptoms, followed by a general listlessness and financial fatigue. For some people, the buildup of deposits is so serious that it leads to financial death (bankruptcy). For others, an early warning is the start of recovery. With a proper diet—budgeting and adherence to sound spending fundamentals—a full recovery may be possible.

Debtabetes

While the buildup of bad debt increases your chance of financial stroke, a poor financial diet can lead to Debtabetes, which is most serious and can eventually lead to amputation of an arm or leg by a creditor (read the fine print in your loan agreement carefully). Debtabetes manifests itself as your inability to break down and eliminate debt because of insufficient cash flow or financial insulin. What most people don't know is that Debtabetes doesn't just limit our ability to process starchy and sugary consumer debt and spending; it also affects the ability to process wholesome spending. Regulation and direction of our financial insulin or cash flow are the key to being financially fit and avoiding Debtabetes. Debtabetes arises from a consumer's inability to manage his or her money supply efficiently. Being debt-obese involves no more than poor money management, due to a combination of habits and environment. How can we allow this to happen? Simple. There is no problem until there is a problem. We don't see the problem until much later on in life. Current cash flow takes care of today without a thought for tomorrow. The invisible harm of not including your future in your spending is setting the stage for an eventual catastrophe. For a fact sheet on Debtabetes as a downloadable PDF, go to www.debtabetes.org.

Debtabetes type 1 assumes you are born in debt. In America we do not come into the world owing for our parents' debts, unless you count a newborn's share of the national debt. This amounts to about $24,000 for every child born in 2004.

Debtabetes type 2. Far worse than owing for their share of the national debt, many young people are harmed further by inheriting their parents' poor financial hygiene. Debtabetes type 2 is typically an environmental disease. The Debtabetes-affected population I am discussing has Debtabetes type 2, which is caused by debt obesity from poor financial habits and the buildup of bad debt. Debtabetes type 2 is also known as adult-onset Debtabetes because it is acquired through poor habits and is not hereditary.

For Debtabetes treatment there is no magic pill—you must change your spending and savings habits to recover. If a pill could be developed, I would recommend a name of Myplansaphalin. Perhaps the side effects would include clear thinking and the desire to develop a workable plan for your life.

Good Debt. By definition, good debt builds wealth. You will have slower financial growth without good debt, although, you could argue, much safer growth. Good debt allows you to leverage your savings and increase your net worth through wise investments. This opportunity for growth, however, has the peril of an equal opportunity for loss. Imprudent investments, as well as relying on someone else to do your thinking for you, are recipes for disaster.

Good debt is debt on assets that provide a cash flow exceeding the amount of the debt service. This is usually a monthly amount. For example, if you have borrowed money to purchase a rental property or a mortgage receivable (where people pay you) and the amount of the income exceeds the debt service by a reasonable amount, that is considered good debt. Money you lend or, more specifically, money others owe you might also be considered good debt. In fact, I would NOT directly lend money, especially to friends. Direct lending is when you give cash to the borrower. It is far better to get yourself educated and buy existing debt secured by real estate.

There are many advantages to buying existing debt. One is that you will have a payment history to evaluate. What you are really buying is an assignment of the right to collect the debt. Here are the basics:

1. Negotiate the purchase (assignment) of a mortgage and note from an owner (home seller or lender) of the mortgage and note that is collecting them.
2. Verify the payer's information, insurance, and appraisal on the security.
3. Have a complete title search and assignment prepared by a competent attorney.
4. Never buy the mortgage if you would hesitate to own the collateral at the price of the assignment plus costs of foreclosure and loss of income while you foreclose.

Where do you find a note and mortgage to buy? Look for someone who has sold his home and accepted part of the payment as cash and part as a note and mortgage secured by the home he sold. If the buyer does not pay, the owner can file a foreclosure action against both the buyer and the property. Let's suppose that for the past five years you have saved 15 percent of your income and now have over $50,000 in the bank at 3 percent and would like a better return (this $50,000 could include your IRA funds too). Mr. Seller had his home for sale five years ago and accepted an offer of $100,000 for the home. The terms were as follows: Mr. Buyer to put $40,000 cash down (equity from his former home) and Mr. Seller to carry a first mortgage of $60,000 at 9 percent interest based on a twenty-year amortization with the entire balance due in ten years. Mr. Seller accepted. Now, five years later, he wants to go into business with his brother-in-law and open a photocopy shop. So he would like to sell (assign) his mortgage and note to someone else for a lump-sum payment. Here's the math on the note:

N (number of payments)	% (rate)	Payment	Present value	Future value (balloon)
240 (original)	9%	$539.84	$60,000	$42,615
180 (remaining)	9%	$539.84	$53,224	$42,615

If you purchase an assignment of Mr. Seller's mortgage and note for $43,000, you will earn about 15 percent on your investment and have all of your money returned in five years. There are many variations possible on this example; I will post at least three more on the www.gooddebt.com Web site. Click on the chapter link that says "The Debt Effects" and then click on "Buy a Mortgage." In case you haven't guessed, *owning* debt, not *owing* debt, is a way to become wealthy.

How could this example use good debt? Suppose that you can buy the above mortgage and note for $43,000. The problem is that you have only about $20,000 to invest (maybe even less). Further, suppose that you have done all of the due diligence and found that it's a solid deal. Borrow the other $23,000 from a bank or a private source secured by the mortgage you are buying. Most conventional lenders won't understand, so you may need to be creative or perhaps borrow from a friend's pension fund. If your friend is struggling to get 5 percent in his pension fund, he might enjoy 9 percent from you and your new asset. Borrow $23,000 at 9 percent, which is six percentage points less than your rate of return.

Other Good Debt?

Sometimes money for education or to start a business is considered a good debt, though debt for education can be very hard to quantify. Good debt is not really "a kind of" debt; it is a result. You may think of it as return on investment—a ratio of what you put in to what you get out. I imagine that if you spent (borrowed) $45,000 to go to law school and as a result you increased your income very significantly over its present level, that's a good debt. But if you became just another mediocre starving attorney, you would have a bad debt on your hands. So too, if you borrowed $90,000 to buy a rental property and the income exceeded the outgo by a comfortable amount, you would consider that good debt. If you failed to rent it or didn't collect the rents, it would be a bad debt. Good debt is also a result measurement, not just a type of debt.

I am amazed at how many folks will not consider borrowing $10,000 to buy a $15,000 or $20,000 mortgage receivable, yet would sign a note for sixty months on a vehicle that will lose half or more of its value within twenty-four months.

Again, you should not invest in something you know little or nothing about. While the upside of investing in mortgages can be great (see resources at www.gooddebt.com), the risks for the untrained are equally great. Train and educate yourself to recognize these good debt opportunities. This book will help.

I am often asked, "Isn't the mortgage on my home a good debt?" It usually is. Strictly speaking, a personal home is not a producing asset (I know, this goes against what most people believe). Some financial advisers argue that your home is only a store of wealth and not an asset at all.

Rather than argue that a personal residence is not an investment, let me give you an exception you can probably accept: a monthly housing cost that does not exceed the cost of renting a suitable dwelling is, while not a good debt, at the least **neutral debt.**

Typically, your home does not produce income and therefore is not considered a good debt. With a little training and effort, however, you can learn how to purchase a home substantially below its market value, thereby reserving a profit for yourself going in. The neutral debt rule assumes, of course, that you are not renting a $2,000-a-month home in a city where there are plenty of $1,200-a-month homes in safe, reasonably desirable neighborhoods—that you are not seeking a mansion on a bungalow budget.

> *The appeal and peace of mind in having your house paid for will likely outweigh anything you can make by keeping it leveraged.*

Most of the financial advisers who say that a home is not a good investment suggest that you should use your home's equity to leverage into other investments. This can be a particularly risky thing to do. If your investments don't work out, you could lose your home.

For most people, borrowing against their personal home will lead to more problems than it cures. I do not recommend it. The appeal and peace of mind in having your house paid for will likely outweigh anything you can make by keeping it leveraged. It's hard to put a price on peace of mind. Conversely, it's hard to truly appreciate peace of mind until you no longer have it.

The Path

So where do the four debt effects lead you? If you ignore them, you may allow unhealthy ambition and greed to take hold of your life. Ultimately, this financial monster can destroy your comfort and joy, because of the exhaustion and stress of trying to maintain a lifestyle that adds nothing permanent to your character or well-being—not to mention your financial statement.

Mom and Dad

The family is the first and most important training ground for youth. Usually if young adults are broke and confused, it's a sign that the parents are broke and confused or missing in action. It is possible to learn money-management lessons late in life, as I was forced to, but if you do not take the time and invest the patience required to learn delayed gratification, record keeping (tracking and tabulation), and prudent investing, you will be a part of the hapless majority of Americans living in relative poverty in their old age.

> *Usually if young adults are broke and confused, it's a sign that the parents are broke and confused or missing in action.*

In *Home*, Samuel Smiles said it this way: "If they have enjoyed the advantage of neither the home nor school, but have been allowed to grow up untrained, untaught, and undisciplined, then woe to themselves—woe to the society of which they form part."

The path to freedom from the four debt effects begins with your self-training as early as possible. Have you ever purchased something and regretted it later? I sure have. Let's move on to the next chapter, "Emotional Hostage: How Do I Get Free from Me?"

Points to Ponder

- It is natural to indulge in illusions of unearned hope. No one is coming to the rescue! You must develop your own plan. You must choose liberty or debt.
- Henry Taylor, in *Notes from Life* (1847), wrote, "A right measure and manner in getting, saving, spending, giving, taking, lending, borrowing, and bequeathing would almost argue a perfect man."
- In its early stages, debt causes no pain. On the contrary, the insidiousness of debt lies in the very fact that it gives its victims temporary pleasure. Sign and drive! No payments until next year! EZ payments!
- Credit to the untrained appetite distorts reality. It affords the emotions vast avenues to explore. Credit allows emotions to trump math—stretching our purchases long into the future and reducing the "right-now cost" to a few dollars a month.
- Review the four debt effects.
  Loss of freedom
  Loss of cash flow
  Loss of time
  Loss of opportunities
- *The invisible hand of debt* always operates.
- P. T. Barnum wrote, "Debt robs a man of his self-respect and makes him almost despise himself."
- Many people have a form of wealth, but deny its power, through lack of discipline and unbridled desire. It is impossible to become wealthy while consumption is near 100 percent.
- When emphasis (in education) is placed on what you feel to

the exclusion of what you know, it plays right into the hands of the merchants that hire agencies to design sophisticated ad campaigns that take advantage of this tendency to feel rather than think.

- You can consider the differences between good debt and bad debt to be much like the differences between good cholesterol and bad cholesterol. Remember, whether an obligation is good or bad debt is based on the results of borrowing—not just whether you call it good or bad debt. Just because a loan involves real estate, it's not automatically a good debt.
- The buildup of bad debt increases your chance of a financial stroke; a poor financial diet can lead to Debtabetes. Cash flow is the financial insulin you need to survive. According to the American Savings Education Council, less than one-third of us are saving enough for retirement. Are you pre-Debtabetes?

Chapter Two
Emotional Hostage:
How Do I Get Free from Me?

Hold on. I still have one good foot!

The ten-second lesson: "You are strong if you conquer others; you are mighty if you conquer self." —Lao Tzu

The Debt Devil places a bid for your emotions long before you awake each morning. He instructs his minions of Madison Avenue to engage your hydraulics of emotion, thus keeping you from seeing the difference between good and bad debt.
— Jon Hanson

It was a beautiful spring afternoon. I had been on the phone several times that day regarding a black XKE convertible. I drove to the seller's house, a nice brick ranch home with a long, long, concrete driveway leading to a six-car garage. The Jaguar was positioned as part of the seller's marketing strategy—in the sun, gleaming, just waiting for a sucke . . . uh, I mean for *me* to look it over.

From the moment I pulled up and saw the sun glistening across the shiny black hood of the car, and somewhere between the sparkle of the wire wheels and my thoughts of the wind whistling through my hair on those romantic evening drives, I knew that I was going to buy that car. Besides, the Debt Devil whispered in my ear, "This will show *'them.' They* will know you have arrived." I was dealing with emotions from so long ago, I couldn't even remember who "they" were supposed to be, yet my will obediently yielded to my emotions and I chucked reason and common sense overboard. The Debt Devil didn't even need to encourage me. I was in emotional free fall without a parachute. I had left it at home on the shelf next to my common sense.

Too Late

I looked at the car and immediately knew that I wanted it, even though all reasoning in the back of my mind screamed faintly, "No! No!" Out front, my emotional self said, "Yes! Yes!" My past of deprivation conspired with my greed for a better life. I was a hostage to my own emotions.

A meeting was convened in my mind. The *Emotions Committee* meeting took only a few seconds. Boy, were they ready! The *Immediate Gratification Task Force* had a prepared list with every reason and every question answered as to why I should have this car. *Delayed Gratification* as well as *Long-Range Planning and Discipline* decided not to speak after seeing *Reason and*

Common Sense shouted down. Over muted protests, the decision was certain. After all, I deserved it, didn't I? Those on the *Long-Range Planning and Discipline Committee* shook their heads and murmured among themselves, "Why would he do that? This is not on the long-range growth plan. This is a huge setback!" They smiled quietly and winked—they knew the Jaguar was to offer a major learning lesson. Like any fundamental, the lesson was always there. I just needed to learn it and then accept it. What happened to my reasoned, rational self? I simply wasn't prepared to handle my emotions, especially in an argument they had been waiting to present for years. I lost the argument with my better self.

Without the Sizzle, Few Steaks Are Sold

While looking at the car, I began to infer things in the transaction that weren't there. The car turned out to be a whole lot of sizzle—and a very tough steak to swallow. In fact, I chewed on it for about five years. This car was not so much a good or bad decision as it was a totally stupid decision. It signified my official status as a hypocrite. Money that went to the Jaguar could have been used for debt reduction or creating a positive cash flow by combining the money with good debt. Most every bad debt decision starts wrapped in the warm glow of emotion. Emotion is the spoonful of sugar that helps you swallow a lot of things that aren't good for you. The main ingredient in all advertising is sugary emotion.

I admit to being quite taken by the seller's whole setting. Not that I lived in a dump, but it was too easy to think if I had *that* car, maybe, just maybe, I'd be closer to having *that* seller's life. When I saw the car, I sprang the full length of my chain. Sadly it became clear that the object of my desire was within my reach. Hindsight brings clarity the morning after a cheap fling with your base emotions.

Perhaps you scoff, but sizzle or sex appeal is the basis of most advertising. The implied message is the *real* message. It is not what you get—but what you *think* you get. In the beer ads, you don't see fat slobs belching and yelling at their wives, "Bring me another brewski, baby!" What you see are the beautiful people, laughing, dining, meeting attractive members of the opposite sex, and seemingly living a life you may only dream of. But remember, they are actors, kind of like the guy selling the Jaguar.

> *Hindsight brings clarity the morning after a cheap fling with your base emotions.*

What advertiser would dare show the underbelly of the beast? Reality is a tough sale and reality is not what they sell—that's my point.

It Doesn't Get Any Better Than This?

Let's continue on the beer ads for a minute. Have you ever seen an ad where the dad is out drinking and doesn't spend time with his family? No? We don't see ads that show the family savings being whizzed down a urinal at the corner pub. Consider a beer ad with the family at the local police station bailing Dad out of jail for DUI—that will never happen. Well, maybe Mothers Against Drunk Driving (MADD) would run that ad.

This day, however, the seller of the Jaguar wasn't disclosing the narrow market or the sickness (regret) he probably had from this car. He was employing the greater-fool theory. (He found his fool and it ended the chain.) He was selling to me the way the beer commercials sell to Joe Average—images of a sunny day, beautiful surroundings, and a big helping of success for everyone! Sadly, it worked, though the entry cost was more than a six-pack of brew.

There Is Wisdom in a Multitude of Counselors

During the Jaguar purchase I did not seek any counsel. Why? Looking back, I have to admit that I did not want anyone to tell me not to buy the car. These were all subconscious thoughts (actually self-repressed thoughts) that never consciously occurred to me until after the damage was done. I felt like the elderly woman who calls the Better Business Bureau after she has been scammed by a con artist. The fellow at the BBB says, "Why didn't you call us before? You know we are here! We have records on this type of thing." The elderly woman replies, "I was afraid you'd tell me not to do it." So, like the little old lady, I wanted to buy that Jaguar even though I knew deep down in my heart, by just getting in touch with my rational self (my own BBB), I could get the straight scoop. Have you ever heard someone say, "I really shouldn't eat this," while you fear he'll lose a finger shoving the food down his throat? That's emotions overrunning common sense. We all do it in some area of our lives, at least some of the time.

> *During the Jaguar purchase I did not seek any counsel. Why? Looking back I have to admit that I did not want anyone to tell me not to buy the car.*

Emotions Trump Common Sense—the Old, Old Story

This is how the enemy wins. Consider Samson. He had the strength to strangle a lion, yet could not control his desire for a

Philistine woman that led to his demise. Whether your end comes by the "D" for Delilah or for debt, scripture warns, "Be sure your sins will find you out." Before I descend from the pulpit here, let's just say that the enemy (the Debt Devil) is anything counterproductive to your stated objectives. I must further assume for the purpose of this example that your objectives aren't insane. In the battle of good debt versus bad debt, your emotions are a key player. Remember this chapter's opening gambit: "You are strong if you conquer others; you are mighty if you conquer self."

The Old Bump and Pick—Advertising 101

The goal of the seducer (advertiser, seller, or creditor) is to slip his sweet words past your reasoning to achieve his objective. It is the classic scheme where one thief (the advertiser) bumps you to distract you, while his buddy (the merchant) picks your pocket. Without emotional appeal, advertising would be pretty difficult. The appeal can be negative or positive—that is, concentrating on what you get or what you could lose.

> *I saw a television ad with the tagline "Feel rich." Notice that the ad did not say, "Be rich."*

Clearly the path past your reasoning is paved with juicy emotions. It seems that juicy emotions distract the blood flow away from your reasoning capacity. This could explain why an otherwise rational and mature person can spend enormous amounts of time and money on nonproductive or even destructive pursuits. It is probably too strong to call advertising deception, but one thing is for sure: in most instances advertisers must distract you from a plan that is better for you than what they are trying to get you to do. The bump and pick works easiest with those who have no particular plan—the Consumerati. **Your attention is easily gained when you are not on a mission.**

None of us are immune to the siren call of Madison Avenue via television, radio, print media, or the interactive innovation of the World Wide Web. We are called and pulled emotionally from many different directions. If none of these get you, peer pressure may.

Bite Me?

If you allow yourself to be "educated" by sound bites and pretty models (male or female) in ads or even network news, instead of reason, rational thinking, and study, you will be forever at the mercy of your emotions. You become a member of the Consumerati—the hunted instead of a hunter, those who build their lives without blueprints. Think of it this way: either you edit what comes into your mind or the media and advertisers do.

During this past Christmas season, I saw a television ad with the tagline "Feel rich." This is an effective emotional appeal; many people are content to feel rather than to be, even though the feeling doesn't last long. Notice that the ad did not say, "Be rich." Control of your emotions can allow you to "Be rich" by following time-honored principles, not the advice of a merchant's mouthpiece. The Econowise set their agenda and follow it, even while all around them members of the Consumerati commit financial indiscretions one after another.

Proper Perspective

I urge you to create your own awareness filled with things that are spiritually, bodily, and financially healthy for you. Once you have completed *Good Debt, Bad Debt*, you will have a framework to guide you. But it doesn't stop there—this is about management, not cure. Emotional management is a full-time job. It requires your leadership to begin and consistent management to continue.

Jimmy Napier, author of *Invest in Debt*, taught me that—unless you are born very rich—to become wealthy you must have a period of sacrifice. I am not sure if I believed Jimmy in 1982, but Jimmy knew something I didn't—that I would cause the need for my financial sacrifice period or at least the need for the time period to be extended.

The type of sacrifice I am talking about produces the great feeling you get when you promise yourself to do something and then actually do it. This is the definition of resolve: promising yourself that you will do something and refusing to quit until it is finished.

It's not bad to want things or even acquire many things. I'd say that it is bad only if it contradicts your plan for your life. If you have no plan for your life, then, by all means, covet away! Party on!

Without control of your emotions and the ability to operate from a definite plan, you leave your future to chance. Do nothing and you may be left to the marketing plan Madison Avenue provides, assuming you have enough income or credit for advertisers to manipulate you. Without a plan, you are forced to cooperate with the inevitable. The old Rush song says, "If you choose not to make a choice, you still have made a choice." We will cover more on planning later. Let's move on—I'm starting to get emotional.

In one of the interviews Tom Stanley does for *The Millionaire Mind*, he speaks of a Mr. Richards saying, "He understands that leasing a Mercedes does not make you rich." It's certainly easy to rationalize reasons to buy things that are unhealthy for you or your financial future. Emotional spending is easy to get caught up in. The sales pitches for your money can be designed to make absolute sense, but when you strip all of the rhetoric away, the only question you need ask yourself is whether this spending brings you nearer to or farther from your goals.

It costs more to put on an appearance of wealth than to take the steps to actually become wealthy. Wealth is not instant. Delayed gratification is the proper prescription here. This is especially true when you count the cost of financing the appearance of wealth. Certainly I recovered from the Jaguar, but it left little emotional scars. You are fortunate if all you lose in a transaction is a little money. It's far worse to lose your nerve, the ability to try again.

The Pity Pot

I had a friend years ago who had a few bad investments and never tried again. He's now spent twenty-two years on the bench. Could you agree that he is paying a far higher cost than losing a little money? Though once a close friend, I can't be around him now. He is so negative and it looks pretty contagious.

It would have been far more costly for me to dwell on my loss on the Jaguar and sit on the sideline for the past few years. Not that I don't have an occasional pity party for myself. Currently, I try to limit my pity parties to twenty minutes and then figure out what I learned and move on.

> *"No one is worthless, honey. Anyone can at least be a good bad example."*

If you must experience self-pity, please do it alone and tell no one. It can be highly contagious to the unvaccinated. I am vaccinated and will either cut your story short or take notes for future writing. If you have a really miserable story, I may want you to sign a release so I can use your story in print as negative inspiration. Most of the negative stuff you hear is rather common to mankind, though the purveyors of negative rhetoric are certain that no one in the world has ever had it as bad as they have. The well-trained mind will ask, What can I learn from this, how do I avoid this happening to me? My mother used to say, "No one is worthless, honey. Anyone can at least be a good bad example."

Mom was right. It's a lot easier to learn from some poor sap's experience than to volunteer for that tour of duty yourself!

Negative Virus—Are You a Carrier?

Spreading your grief may only infect others or keep them from trying. The recently popular buzz on the Web is viral marketing. Dr. Ralph Wilson says, "In brick and mortar businesses, this is known as *word-of-mouth.*" I say negative thinking is the greatest viral marketing plan ever devised by the old Debt Devil. It costs nothing initially (except your future) to join and it's easy to recruit victims. Many people are actually predisposed to look for this sort of thing. If you've ever seen someone draw all those circles and explain how you can make millions selling soap or phone cards, then just apply that math to your negative thinking.

ATTRIBUTES OF VIRAL MARKETING

1. **Is free to catch**—Whether it's an actual cold virus, a product, a negative message, or a positive message, the transfer is free.
2. **Effortlessly transfers to others**—Viruses spread only when they are easy to catch. Shake hands with someone

who has a cold, forward an e-mail, tell a friend—it is a nearly effortless transfer.

3. **Scales easily from small to large**—To spread rapidly, a virus replicates itself with ease. In the e-mail example, an infinite number of e-mails or negative stories may be generated at no cost to the initiator of the virus.

4. **Exploits common motivations**—Motivations include to be funny, to be loved, to fulfill a greed, to fulfill a need, to annoy others, to create fear, or to feel better by pulling others down.

5. **Uses existing communication channels**—Person-to-person communication spreads the common cold; e-mail and downloading files spread the marketing on the net; word of mouth spreads joy or misery.

6. **Takes advantage of others' resources**—The cold virus travels on someone else's hand; the e-mail or downloaded file prints on someone else's paper; the virus travels by virtue of someone else's time and effort.

This bulletin just in! You may also apply viral marketing to positive pursuits. The same math prevails. Though not everyone knows how to accept a positive message, you will be surprised how many do, and some may be happy to try something new. Truly, there may be more negative than positive "carriers" out there. You will always find those who enjoy having someone to be miserable with, but some will prefer a positive message.

What Did I Learn?

The Jaguar fiasco was many years ago and today I jokingly refer to this as a $15,000 seminar on Emotions Management 101. Don't laugh. Think of the cost of your own lessons. You'd think that for tuition spent, this would have been a graduate-level course, but the lesson was very basic. Prerequisite courses are often useful building blocks for advanced learning. For a modest price, I did the thesis work on the Newton-Hanson Theory: **"In a financial transaction, every unbridled emotion has an equal and opposite dulling effect on common sense."**

I am serious in saying that the lesson learned has been worth more than the dollars lost. For you wisecrackers out there, it would not be twice as valuable for me to repeat this lesson! I never discuss good debt versus bad debt without including emotional management. How could I?

> *"Not to have a mania for buying things is to possess a revenue."*

What hurt the most in the Jaguar fiasco was that I did not have control of my emotions. I allowed myself to be taken in. Through my own actions, I gave up part of my assets to feed my ego. It is a terrible feeling to be conned out of your money and, after a thorough investigation, find that you are the culprit. Had I hired a detective, I would have found out more quickly that I was the thief—even Geraldo Rivera could have solved this one.

I have no particular animus toward the seller of the XKE, though I have clenched my teeth a few times when I think of the transaction. Recently I removed his picture from my dartboard. He did not force me to buy the car; I accept full responsibility. As a bonus I learned why all the jokes about British cars are essentially true.

Allowing my emotions to think for me cost me a bundle. The story would not be even worthy of note if this were my only screwup. Unfortunately, my lapses have extended to other areas also. Mind you, for most people, cars are losers and a constant source of expense. However, I was accustomed to making money buying and selling cars as a hobby and for profit. I am usually selling to an emotional buyer, not being one! So, as I entered into my journal a few years after this self-inflicted trauma, "When I saw the topless Jaguar glistening in the sun, sitting in front of the seller's six-car garage, my emotions ran high and financial acuity plunged low—I just kind of became the guy I should have been looking for and took advantage of myself." I try to keep this in the proper perspective now. It was a learning event.

Remember, "You are strong if you can conquer others; you are mighty if you can conquer self." The battle for control of your emotions is with yourself! Cicero said, "Not to have a mania for buying things is to possess a revenue." Emotional spendthrifts are nothing new. All of history is replete with examples. I call these spendthrifts the Consumerati—those who become slaves to their own desires. An important key to your financial future is gaining control of your emotions. Those with control of their emotions along with a few other fundamentals belong to the elite group, the Econowise.

Understand what the Debt Devil and Madison Avenue are trying to get you to do. You can go along with their bump and pick or take charge of your thinking. In the preceding sentence, please notice the word *you*. It is still your choice—free will is still free. While it may sound like I am railing against Madison Avenue, I am not. Advertisers are doing what merchants have hired them to do: sell products—lots of them. The battle I am talking about is with a much more formidable foe—yourself!

Even when debt is not accruing, we may engage in McSpending—promiscuous spending that we don't realize counts until later when we calculate the cost. These are the small amounts of spending we don't often account for. The five or ten dollars a day of petty cash leakage can add up to more than half a million dollars over twenty or thirty years. McSpending can be anything from the $3.50 Starbucks coffee to expensive lunches, while our IRA or retirement account lags.

In the detour from the plan for my life, I acquired a loser, but, worse than that, I deluded myself into thinking that the pernicious Jaguar was an asset. The emotional decision I made to purchase the Jaguar instead of investing the money by paying down debt was a big mistake. I have always prided myself on being able to tell my assets from a hole in the ground, but that day it was as if I had a common sense bypass. I deluded myself into thinking that I would actually make money on this loser. Self-delusion is the most dangerous type of delusion, because whatever you wish to believe is what you're convinced is true.

High Stakes

Few things in life can cost you more than unrestrained emotions. You stand at the edge of a good-debt–versus–bad-debt decision each time you let your emotions make decisions for you in money-handling situations. My friend Jimmy Napier taught me, "At every negotiating gambit, you have the opportunity to make or spend more than at any other moment of your life." Once you add in emotions and "media-induced coveting," you are at a severe disadvantage.

I am still recovering from the self-inflicted bruises sustained from decisions made years ago. Yet we can't live in the past. Regret is a useless emotion; it robs from your present and cripples your tomorrow.

I paraphrase Jim Rohn from a Nightingale-Conant tape I heard years ago: regret is a useless emotion. Spend a few minutes on it and you begin the economic bone cancer that leads to death. You'll end up hauling yourself off to the financial desert, where you can choke on the dust of your own regret.

Full Frontal Clarity

At some point in your life, you have the sudden realization that you would be much further ahead in life and free if not for the debt and obligations that you have collected along the way. When you notice that enough money has passed through your hands and that just 5 or 10 percent of it would by now have grown to a fortune, then you are ready to begin learning. *The best lessons in life can be learned but not taught.* Sadly, they can be ignored too.

Brian Tracy in *The Psychology of Achievement* says, "Eight-five percent of your happiness comes from how successfully you can interact with other people." If emotional intelligence, working toward your goal, delayed gratification, and building your knowledge base a little each day are so important, why don't we hear more about them? It seems that each millionaire's story highlights what the millionaire will do with his money or how he got his money. These are all fine stories, but more useful may be a story of what was going on inside the millionaire while he made his money.

> *The best lessons in life can be learned but not taught.*

Being emotionally successful means knowing and applying fundamentals. *Fundamentals are principles that act in a consistent manner independent of your understanding, action, or inaction.* The fundamental of compound interest will work for you or against you regardless of your understanding. Money is no respecter of persons; it works equally for or against all who will give it employment. With consumer debt, aka bad debt, compound interest charges work against you. With prudent investments, compound interest will work for you. Compound interest, like gravity, operates either for or against you.

Paper-Train Yourself

Writing things down is a fundamental you should apply that will always increase clarity and recall. Commit to memory the well-known creed, "The faintest ink is better than the best memory." You do not need to understand electricity to flip the light switch and receive the benefit of light. Take notes. You are living the test, and thankfully it's an open-book exam.

Whatever you take time to hold up to the light, to read, to absorb, to think deeply about, ask, "How could this help me, help my family, my situation, my work, my finances? Is this profitable instruction?" If it is not profitable or edifying, why are you doing it?

Since you may implement only what you are aware of, your awareness will determine your level of success. If we agree with the old adage that your attitude controls your altitude, then I hope that you'll agree with me when I say that your awareness controls your possibilities.

> *Fundamentals are principles that are time tested and proved by common sense. They will endure beyond our lives and those of our descendants.*

In Chapter 6 ("What If You Live?"), I will expand on having a life plan and a job replacement plan. Self-control and self-discipline are declining commodities in America. The big sucking sound we hear is not jobs heading to Mexico or India, but the sound of a vacuum created by people trying to live their life devoid of the fundamental skill of handling money.

Fundamentals are principles that are time tested and proved by common sense. They will endure beyond our lives and those of our descendants. What are we teaching our children? It has been said that a boy listens to what his father says until age eleven, and then he does what his father does. You can explain away your words, but not your actions. Are your actions consistent with your words? This is a constant source of grief for many people. Can you daily reconcile your words with your actions? We all know brilliant people with an abundance of talent who seem to never move ahead. Their talent can't be implemented if they lack discipline. The wisdom of the ages comes to this: seek wisdom, discipline, and discernment.

Have you noticed that the word *rationalize* has the sound of "rational lies"? People lie mostly to themselves. They think "someday," "when I," "then I will," and other delusions. These are all mild sedation for the mind trying to ration lies to itself to explain away actions or inactions. "Someday I'll" or "I'll try" is the cheap drug people use to excuse themselves from sincere effort. Brian Tracy says, *"I'll try* is excusing failure in advance."

Here are a few fundamentals for debt and emotion control:

1. Get paper-trained! When you think about decisions, always do it on paper. High emotions lower financial acuity. If it doesn't make sense on paper, it probably doesn't make sense in practice. Planning is often the highest-return thing you can do.
2. Learn to discern when emotions are swaying your decision-making ability. The Newton-Hanson Theory says, "In a financial transaction, every unbridled emotion has an equal and opposite dulling effect on common sense."
3. Think of *rationalize* as "rational lies." Who are you lying to? Probably yourself. Many (like me) don't like record keeping because it is not fun and it tends to bring too much clarity to how we are doing. It is better to adapt Patrick Henry's attitude about freedom to finances: "For

my part, whatever anguish of spirit it may cost, I am willing to know the whole truth; to know the worst, and to provide for it."

4. Be consistent. Keep your actions consistent with your words. Improve your words and actions.

5. Self-select. Set your priorities and purpose or someone else will set them for you. You must self-select or take leftovers.

Be Careful What You Wish For

Many work to acquire luxuries, and then become slaves to those luxuries. We are born free yet entrap ourselves in a web of debt and time obligations that make us voluntary slaves or at least pitiful employees of our creditors. This is nothing new. Through all of my reading, research, and informal interviews with debtors great and small, a recurring theme was found: they all lamented how much time and money they had spent on trivial items that were long gone and forgotten.

Set Priorities

Each of us must decide on our priorities. At the local pool hall, Joe Debtor is trying to borrow $500—he says it's to pay his wife Ima's hospital bills. The businessman says to Joe, "I can't lend you $500. You'll just drink it all up." "No, no, no," says Joe. "You don't understand. Drinking money I got!"

Joe may not be a good credit risk, but he certainly has his priorities straight. In Chapter 5 ("I Don't Know About My Past: But My Future Is Spotless"), I talk about how my family came up with $600 in 1965 to buy a color TV, yet we never came up with $600 to invest or even buy a house. And in 1965, $600 down would buy a house (it can today also). Are your priorities like Joe Debtor's?

I have talked to many Joes and Imas over the past years. Priorities are funny things. Other people's priorities are lame. Ours are the golden calves of priorities. The last Joe I talked to lamented that he couldn't put even $1,000 a year into a Roth IRA. In casual conversation I asked about a program I knew that was on a cable network. He told me all about it and many others! Perhaps a private investigator's report would have said, "Subjects: Joe and Ima Debtor spend at least $1,500 a year on cable, HBO, and pay-per-view without regard to their financial future." I assume that this would be a conservative estimate.

Actually, Joe is correct! He can't afford to invest in a Roth IRA—but HBO money he's got. One common characteristic of all people in bondage is that they lie. The drunk has his reasons; the overeater has his reasons; the gambler and the debt impaired too have their reasons. They have rational lies (rationalize).

> *When you allow yourself to be led by your emotions, you are not in control.*

Do the Right Thing

If you do what is right, your feelings (emotions) will follow. This may be the toughest lesson to learn. It is the toughest lesson I am still learning. Many people fall into the trap of following their emotions. When you allow yourself to be led by your emotions, you are not in control. This is because you have abdicated control to your emotions. All sales training teaches salespeople to appeal to prospects' emotions, not to get caught up in unproductive discussions about affordability. Car dealers prefer to talk in terms of easy monthly payments rather than the total price of the vehicle.

A hallmark of the Consumerati is their proclivity for delusion. They are apt to rationalize and create many reasons for unsound spending. Some just give up altogether. Have you ever heard anyone say, "I prefer delusion to reality"?

The Consumerati believe in what they can see and feel now. The main difference between the Consumerati and the Econowise is their view of the future.

The Consumerati believe in what they can see and touch now. They have little confidence in tomorrow—this is why they are so willing to pledge or mortgage it. The Consumerati seek immediate **happiness**—even if it's only temporary.

The Econowise believe in the future—and that a knowable future can be reached. They do the math and then trust the math. The Econowise seek lasting **joy**.

Traveling at the Speed of Debt

We have accelerated consumption and the Consumerati lifestyle with speed, efficiency, and technology—but have outrun common sense and wisdom. The Econowise understand that fundamentals never change and that only by adherence to these time-honored fundamentals will we be successful. The Econowise take a ten- , twenty- , or even fifty-year view of their financial life.

FAQ—How Can I Be Free If I Don't Do What I Want?

Question: how can I be free if I don't follow my inner emotions? Answer: freedom is found in self-discipline. What? I know it is counter to everything popular culture teaches you. Freedom is found in restraint. Only through conscious choice can we begin to control our outcomes. You must self-select. When we follow our feelings we actually give up freedom. We become slaves to our feelings and, in the end, our actions are at the mercy of our moods, our money, or the urging of an advertiser. After all, you deserve the best. Don't you?

This is a most unpredictable path. You may get a similar result selecting a spouse based totally on emotion without the benefit and burden of common sense, reasoning, and measuring compatibility. You must decide what religion to follow, whom to marry, and what level of financial health you wish to obtain. The Consumerati refuse responsibility and are given over to their emotions until finally they collapse under the weight (debt) of their own desires.

> *If we follow our emotions we have given up freedom— then we are slaves to our emotions.*

Eyes Wide Open

Isaac Singer wrote, "We have to believe in free will. We've got no choice." Actually, free will allows us the choice of embracing pretty much no plan. We may just go with the flow—or the three I's: indifference, immediacy, and ignorance. This same free will allows us to embrace a plan and a predictable promise, which I call the three Ds: discipline, deferral, and discernment. I am asking not for blind faith but for a faith with eyes wide open. You have the free will to do the math and record keeping honestly for your situation as we proceed. Certainly it's easier to put down this book and pick up the remote control or say, "I will do this later." You have free will to do whatever you wish— just do it with your eyes wide open.

Learn to discern when you are being led by your emotions. When confronted or compromised emotionally, simply ask if it is really in your long-term best interest to go with your emotions. They aren't always wrong. Just be aware of who or what is whetting and training your appetites. Remember the Econowise question: does this spending (or action) move me nearer to or farther from my goals?

Points to Ponder

- The Newton-Hanson Theory says, "In a financial transaction, every unbridled emotion has an equal and opposite dulling effect on common sense."
- It is a terrible feeling to be conned out of your money and, after a thorough investigation, find that you are the culprit.
- Question: how can I be free if I don't follow my inner emotions? Answer: freedom is found in self-discipline. Only through conscious choice, a plan, can we begin to control our outcomes. Following your emotions leaves you captive to an unpredictable master.
- Hindsight brings clarity the morning after a cheap fling with your base emotions.
- The well-trained mind will ask, What can I learn from this, how do I avoid letting this happen to me? My mother used to say, "No one is worthless, honey. Anyone can at least be a good bad example."
- The goal of the seducer (advertiser-seller-creditor) is to slip words past your reasoning to achieve an objective. It is the classic scheme where one thief (the advertiser) bumps you to distract, while his buddy (the merchant) picks your pocket.
- Jimmy Napier taught me, "At every negotiating gambit, you have the opportunity to make or spend more than at any other moment of your life."
- Money is no respecter of persons. It works equally for or against all who give it employment.
- Insanity is when you desperately want to do something detri-

mental to your well-being. It is insanity to have well-defined goals and then not follow them. To avoid the discomfort caused by setting and writing out goals, many decide to never begin.

- Think of it this way: either you edit what comes into your mind or the media and advertisers do.
- The more emotionally based you allow your decisions to be, the more bad debt you will likely accrue.
- The more rationally based your decisions are, the more likely you are to avoid bad debt.

Chapter Three

Burn Rate:
Spending, Not Income, Determines Wealth

We can't make you the loan, Mr. Johnson. And after looking
at your credit report, we'd like to have our calendar back.

*The ten-second lesson: "I've got all the money I'll ever need, if
I die by four o'clock."*
— Henny Youngman

For some, a job that provides for all their present needs may give
them the illusion of wealth. Mix this together with a little easy-
to-get consumer debt, and present needs or desires seem to expand. Just as work tends to expand to the time allotted,
spending, without restraint, expands to the amount of money
available—or even beyond. It is hard to see spending as a problem while all of your existing needs and many desires are being

met. Truly, we can't see the problem for the solution. The tendency to confuse income with wealth is near an epidemic level among Americans. Income is like a moving river; wealth is like a lake or reservoir. Stored income is wealth; spent income may not even bring fond memories.

This illusion of wealth, together with a genuine unconcern for the future, persists exactly because many people are so well satisfied in their daily desires—they do not see the wisdom of spending less than they make. Less than 5 percent of the population will take the time to have a written plan for their life. Perhaps committing their financial life to paper would be too sobering. If you consistently spend all you make, you will never be set financially. The biographies of great men from Ben Franklin to Warren Buffett will bear out this fact.

A job or your own business can create wealth for you only if a part of your earnings is taken captive and made to work for you. Bad debt early in life can set a pattern of nearly perpetual spending and borrowing that can lead to your financial ruin.

> *Income is a like a moving river; wealth is like a lake or reservoir. Stored income is wealth; spent income may not even bring fond memories.*

Premature Affluence

Part of this problem is a pattern of early debt we may acquire from the adult role models in our life, and part may be what University of Michigan researcher Jerald Bachman calls *premature affluence.* Says Bachman, "In the absence of payments for rent, utilities, groceries, and the many other necessities routinely provided for by parents, the typical student is likely to find that most or all of his/her earnings are available for discretionary spending. And given that many are earning in excess of $200 per month, it seems likely that some will experience what I've come to call 'premature affluence'—*affluence* because $200 or more per month represents a lot of 'spending money' for a high school student, and *premature* because many of these individuals will not be able to sustain that level of discretionary spending once they have to take on the burden of paying for their own necessities."

Since this study was published in 1983, I am sure you could more than double these figures. My informal survey of high school waitresses and waiters found some saying they make about $500 a month part-time. One waitress, age eighteen and still living at home, told me that she earns $600 to $800 a month for fifteen to twenty hours a week of work.

Some students acquire a taste for name brands and expensive necessities. Then, after college, when the full expense of a household begins, many choose bad debt to sustain their lifestyles rather than downshift to no-name brands. At $8 a gallon, no wonder Evian is naive spelled backward.

> *Moving a desire to the need list is a basic Consumerati technique.*

It is good that young people are working and earning part of their keep. The majority of the small sample I informally interviewed were paying their way through college while working. The problem can develop when we allow (by example or neglect) our youth to train an appetite that may lead them to financial slavery. I left home just before I turned seventeen. I remember thinking a year later about the good old days when I was making $90 a week, was living at home, and had money to burn. Once I had to pay for my own housing, utilities, food, dating, cars, and clothes, my rose-colored glasses were shattered.

Who's That Lurking in the Bushes?

Consumer debt, like all traps, is easy to get into and hard to get out of. To paraphrase Proverbs 1:11, the Bible warns us, "Beware of those who lie in wait for innocent blood." Perhaps we should say, "Beware of those who lie in wait for naive or ignorant blood"—meaning financial blood, of course. Today it is the advertisers lying in wait for innocent blood. Of course, they don't use a knife or gun—they use emotional appeal. Therefore, it is up to you to choose whether or not to enter into a debt trap. Your best defense here is to deconstruct and deflect the media influences in your life as discussed in Chapter 2 ("Emotional Hostage").

Many confuse needs or necessary expenditures with desires. Each of us has desires that far exceed our actual needs. Moving a desire to the need list is a basic Consumerati technique. They do this in an attempt to justify the spending. Syndicated columnist Cal Thomas wrote, "A need has been redefined to mean a 48-hour want." The dissonance created by stupid spending can be temporarily relieved by people deceiving themselves into believing that the spending is necessary. Trying to satisfy a majority of your desires is a formula for bankruptcy, or extended poverty at the very best.

Defining Burn Rate. Your burn rate is the actual amount of money you spend each month to stay in the same place—your status quo. This includes all fixed costs of living and the impulse buying you do now and then. Your burn rate is the sum total of your financial obligations, plus spending on food, shelter, and any extravagances. Simply said, burn rate is all the money spent that does not increase your wealth. Burn rate is what is consumed and gone forever. Taxes are a major part of your burn rate, together with food, shelter, and transportation.

Meet LERI

You could also think of your burn rate as your *fixed cost of existence*. Only the portion of income in excess of your burn rate can be available to build wealth or attain freedom from toil. There is no secret to becoming wealthy—you must lower your burn rate or increase your income, preferably both. This is easy to remember as the acronym LERI—Lower Expenses or Raise Income. There is nothing else you can do about cash flow. All the MBAs in the world can't come up with a better solution for cash flow. In addition, you must take the difference between burn rate and income and invest it wisely. It is only the portion of your income above burn rate that is available for wealth building or retirement. Let me recap: lower your expenses, raise your income, and do something good with the difference (spread). Lowering your nondeductable expenses is a nontaxable event.

If you are now forty years old, every $100 monthly in excessive burn rate knocks out $132,000 of potential retirement nest egg. Of course, a large portion of your income early on must go to burn rate or the cost of living. What does not have to happen is for you to constantly add to what you call necessities. As your income rises, resist the temptation to ratchet up your lifestyle. Conversely, there is no wisdom in being a penny-pinching miser who starves both body and mind either. What if the onetime $100,000 you saved on education cost you over $100,000 a year for life?

> *As your income rises, resist the temptation to ratchet up your lifestyle.*

The best things in life can be had only with balance and wisdom in choice. We are all given free will, before debt, to choose where our resources will be spent. Once we have debt and large monthly expenses the four debt effects begin to rule. We experience loss of freedom, loss of cash flow, loss of time, and loss of opportunities. In reality, when we spend while in debt, we are spending our creditors' money. They allow us to do this as long as we pay the agreed upon monthly interest and principle. Paying with credit is not really payment in full; it is payment to a third party or directly to a vendor, and the third party or vendor now has a claim on your future earnings.

Balance

Perhaps the goal is to live somewhere between being a miser and being extravagant—somewhere between Scrooge and the average politician. In *Architects of Fate*, Orison Marden relates the following story: "Guy, the London bookseller, and afterward the founder of the great hospital, was a great miser, living in the back part of his shop, eating upon an old bench, and using his counter for a table, with a newspaper for a cloth. He did not marry. One day he was visited by 'Vulture' Hopkins, another well-known miser. 'What is your business?' asked Guy, lighting a candle. 'To discuss your methods of saving money,' was the reply, alluding to the stingy economy for which Guy was famous. On learning Hopkins' business he blew out the light, saying, 'We can do that in the dark.' 'Sir, you are my master in the art,' said the Vulture; 'I need ask no further. I see where your secret lies.'

"We may all laugh at Guy's economy, but it is far better than the extravagance that laughs at it," says Marden. Truly, a reasonable balance is what is needed. If your method of economy is to save money by scrimping on education, record keeping and organization, or healthy eating, then you could be saving for an end you may never reach.

I repeat for effect, if you are forty years of age, every $100 a month you continuously burn costs you over $132,000 at age sixty-five. It costs you because of debt effect 4, loss of opportunity. If you have already burned the money, you can't invest the ashes. Said differently, invest $100 a month for twenty-five years (ages forty to sixty-five, for example) in a mutual fund, mortgage paper, or other investment at only 10 percent, and you will have $132,683. I assume a 10 percent rate here, which is high for savings as of this writing and very low for investing in mortgage paper or other hands-on active investments available to an educated investor. If you doubt the fluctuation of savings rates, read a little history or live awhile. In twenty-two years I have seen savings rates banks offer vary from 2 to 16 percent. The tiny voice of prudence may one day whisper in your ear, "Is it worth $132,000 for cable TV with all the premium channels?" For you math majors, assuming the yield above, what would $1,000 a month (ten times the amount) spared from burn rate and properly directed be in twenty-five years?

The sooner you eliminate the waste, lower your burn rate, and begin an Econowise program, the better. With compound interest assuming the variables above beginning twenty years earlier, your $100 a month would become $1,048,250.

> *"Now here,"* said the Queen, *"it takes all the running you can do to keep in the same place."*

Burn rate is what you consume as in burn up. If you are like me, it sure feels like you are burning the income, doesn't it? Regardless of the emotions of "burning through" your income, it nevertheless is a necessity—to a point. Many with a high burn rate tell me that they feel like they are on a treadmill. Lewis Carroll, in *Alice in Wonderland,* describes the feeling: "Now here," said the

Queen, "it takes all the running you can do to keep in the same place."

If your known burn rate exceeds 90 percent given the inevitable leakage together with "convenient memory bookkeeping," you are probably losing ground. My wealthy friend Bob Teague, Jr., says, "If your outgo exceeds your income, then your upkeep becomes your downfall."

We are creatures of habit and comfort, having all of these customs we become attached to, like eating and having a roof over our head, a nice car or two, and 150 TV channels to view. It's likely, though, that food and shelter are not what is keeping you from getting ahead financially.

Though I have seen people who keep themselves broke trying to live in a starter mansion while they should be in a tract home, it is generally the extras, those supposed "gotta haves," that keep the burn rate in the 95 percent range or higher. In Chapter 1 ("The Debt Effects"), I say that many people have a form of wealth (income), but deny its power through lack of discipline and unbridled desire. These are the self-deluded pretending to be wealthy. Teague calls them "goldbrickers," as they try to project wealth on the surface, but when they are scratched you find the gold is really only gold paint on a common brick.

Can't We Live at a Profit?

It is an accumulation of trinkets and questionable services that monthly leads us to poverty. Few go broke all at once; most go broke over a period of years with the monthly obligations building up not unlike the plaque that builds up in our arteries from a poor diet. The buildup of bad debt operates like weight gain—we grow fat one sticky bun at a time, by treating our bodies like trash cans with hairy lids. We grow obese from shoving too much food down our pie holes—we grow poor from overspending and debt accumulation. Those who live long lives catering to their preferences (gotta haves) at the end of life are lucky to afford the necessities (must haves). If you are a member of the Consumerati, the only way to join the Econowise is by a change of habits—truly a renewing of your mind.

Henry David Thoreau, in *Walden Pond*, describes how he lived on $38 one year. Thoreau's book has a page of his record keeping for the year. I assure you that $38 was a thrifty sum even in his day. Don't dismiss the power of these examples by filtering with sarcasm and fuzzy math. P. T. Barnum mentions Thoreau as an example in his autobiography, *Life of Barnum*. Here are two paragraphs from *Life of Barnum*, written about 1863, as he purposed to live on $600 a year in 1845 while he began to operate the American Museum.

At the very outset, I was determined to deserve success. My plan of economy included the intention to support my family in New York on $600 a year, and my treasure of a wife not only gladly assented, but was willing to reduce the sum to $400, if necessary. Some six months after I had bought the Museum, Mr. Olmsted happened in at my ticket-office at noon, and found me eating a frugal dinner of cold corned beef and bread, which I had brought from home.

"Is that the way you eat your dinner?" he asked.

"I have not eaten a warm dinner, except on Sundays," I replied, "since I bought the Museum, and I never intend to, on a week day, till I am out of debt."

"Ah!" said he, clapping me on the shoulder, "you are safe, and will pay for the Museum before the year is out."

And he was right, for within twelve months I was in full possession of the property as my own, and it was entirely paid for from the profits of the business.

I love the part where Barnum says, "I was determined to deserve success." Are we determined to deserve our success or willing to take whatever life hands us, what falls off the table? John Kenneth Galbraith called this "accommodating poverty." There is a large difference between saying, "I deserve it" and "I shall put myself in a position to deserve it." We are apt to think that the millionaire inherited his or her money or became suddenly wealthy. A careful reading of history will debunk that myth. Most millionaires earned their money, delayed gratification, and controlled their burn rate.

> *Your burn rate as a percentage of income is the most accurate predictor of your eventual success or failure.*

Even if you are blessed with a sudden windfall, it is unlikely that without these money management skills you will be able to retain your wealth. Wealth will only make you more of what you already are. Without the skills of the Econowise, the sudden wealth of the Consumerati will soon migrate back to the Econowise group.

The lesson of both Thoreau and Barnum is that you may simplify, no matter the times. Later in *Life of Barnum*, Barnum says, "The American Museum was the ladder by which I rose to fortune and fame." We must understand that if Barnum had not controlled his burn rate, we would have never heard of him.

We must be aware of our monthly burn rate to make productive use of the information. If you just muttered to yourself, "Where's the mystery? I spend it all!" that's not quite what I had in mind. Certainly it is funny to laugh and joke about your bills, but when the laughter subsides, as it always does, the debt endures.

> *Breaking even is not the goal. If you proceed on this path, you will have nothing for the future.*

If you are using exactly all of your income on burn rate, don't feel bad. Many people use it all like that. But breaking even is not the goal. If you proceed on this path, you will have nothing for the future. Does it occur to you that you are working for free or perhaps just room and board when you save or invest nothing?

Here are some U.S. Bureau of the Census statistics that are commonly batted about by inspirational and financial speakers when they discuss where many folks of retirement age find themselves:

- Ninety percent are partially or totally dependent on government or family.
- Five percent are self-sufficient.
- Four percent are well off.
- One percent are fabulously wealthy.

Burn, Baby, Burn

In 2002, the average family of four, according to our government, made $69,800 per year. This means that such a family will handle more than $2,792,000 as their total forty-year salary, not even considering inflation or career advancement. So the risk of starving is tiny. The real risk is self-inflicted, beginning when we decide what reference group we want to keep up with. I hope you pick the right one! **Your burn rate as a percentage of income is the most accurate predictor of your eventual success or failure financially.** It is accurate to say that burn rate decides fate.

The less you burn, the sooner you can stop working or at

least begin doing what you really want to do. Low burn rate has allowed me to leave real estate and become a full-time writer and speaker. Writing and speaking have always been my passion. For many of us, our passions are pushed aside by the rule of the four debt effects. Isn't the purpose of a job to put you in a position where you don't need a job?

Let's say that I spend all I make. What's the problem? I'll just make more. Again, this is a dangerous school of thought. While you are young and healthy you can always just make more money. But you will run out of something else: time. Besides having the clock run out on you, the optimism of youth must give way to the physical body of old age.

"The supply of time, though gloriously regular, is cruelly restricted," proclaims Arnold Bennett in his 1910 book, *How to Live on Twenty-four Hours a Day*. Bennett continues, "Which of us has not been saying to himself all his life: 'I shall alter that when I have a little more time'?" As you get older, you may notice that you begin to value time more than money. This will be especially true once you begin to accumulate wealth.

The world has unlimited opportunity, but we all have limited time. Think of what you do to generate income. Now hold that picture in your mind. Is it your life's passion? If it is, you are indeed fortunate, but even if it is, there will come a time when you may not be physically able to do what you want. Robert Kiyosaki in *Rich Dad, Poor Dad* wisely says, "A job is a short term solution to a long term problem." On the evening news you may watch aestheticians (they use only statistics that make them look good) pick and choose partial statistics that support their cause or favored program. In *Good Debt, Bad Debt* I urge you to use the real numbers that count—the ones from *your* life. Measure your progress as described in Chapter 6 ("What If You Live?") under the heading "Wealth Metrics."

It is best to arrange your finances so that a portion goes to take care of your future needs. You can begin this process only when you know exactly where, when, and in what amounts your money leaves you. Try saying to your friends, "I choose to have less now so that I can have more later!" Hard work alone cannot create wealth. Wealth is dependent on accumulation.

How Important Is Burn Rate?

Now comes the question that should illuminate the problem. Who is doing better? Is it the Consumerati or the Econowise? Let's stretch an example to the point of the ridiculous, but not so far that it can't illustrate my point. I think in the following example you will easily see the exaggeration and be able to fill in where needed. Here is a fact that neither omits nor exaggerates: it is your burn rate, not your income, that will determine your fate.

Case 1

Here we have a surgeon salaried at $18,000 a month with a burn rate of $17,000. The jumbo mortgage on Dr. Lotta Bucks' minimansion ($5,987 a month) plus taxes totals about $1,200 a month, and insurance is $300 a month. Of course, Doc needs a country club membership at $15,000 a year. In Doc's neighborhood, the Chevrolet Lumina isn't chic. Doc therefore leases a Mercedes at $850 a month. The new wife needs a BMW SUV for $599 a month, and she is not a Wal-Mart shopper for clothes, no sir. Before clothes, professional dues, food, maid, the pool boy Armando (Mrs. Doc really likes him), furnishings, entertaining, and miscellaneous, Doc is pumping out over $10,000 a month.

Don't forget the peer pressure on Doc—a boat, a few jet skis, and exotic vacations are a must. Doc must really work hard to keep Mrs. Doc, Armando, the gardener, and everyone else with a hand out each month happy. The doc can find no peace in his six-thousand-square-foot mansion. With a $900,000 mortgage, he can't even call it his own. Additionally, the first wife (known as Medical School Wife) keeps filing for an increase in her alimony payments, as she would like to be able to afford the services of her own Armando.

Case 2

Joe Average is salaried at $4,200 a month with a burn rate of $2,876 per month. His house payment, including taxes and insurance, is $800 a month. The car is paid for, but he has a truck payment of $299. He also has the usual expenses of eating, transportation, and entertainment. Yet he has a plan to invest $1,200 a month toward retirement. Mrs. Joe makes about $6,000 a year net sewing dresses for dolls that Billy Bob's wife sells at flea markets. Mrs. Joe has decided to save her entire $6,000 each year toward retirement also or maybe buy the house that Billy Bob rents from his uncle for $700 a month.

We will show twenty years of Mrs. Joe's savings, but they will not be included in the comparison with Doc Lotta Bucks' savings. If the surgeon doesn't change his ways, I'd rather be Joe Average. Actually, given Doc Lotta Bucks' relationships (Medical School Wife, Trophy Wife, Armando, and the gang), I think I'd rather be Joe Average. No matter what you make, it is how much you have left over after expenses (or burn rate) that matters.

For the magical purpose of making a point, let's assume that neither one of these guys changes anything for twenty years. That won't happen, but since books are static, let's go with what we have. We will further ignore taxes, divorce, sickness, and midlife craziness that seem common to the population. Doc won't run off with his nurse (again) and Joe won't date his sister-in-law. Let's invest both Doc's and Joe's net income after burn rate in the Rock of Gibraltar—We Got Your Money— Conservative Vulture Mutual Fund. Rock of Gibraltar Funds, in their glossy slick promotions, brag that they average 24.03 percent per annum. There was, too, a lot of fine print that I could not read without a microscope.

Assuming that we understand averages, Zig Ziglar says, "If you have one foot in ice water and the other one in boiling water, on the average you should be comfortable." So just for fun, let us pretend that Rock of Gibraltar could actually pull 12 percent over twenty years. Here's how the investments would look in twenty years:

Number of Monthly Payments	Rate (Yield)	Monthly Investment	Future Value
DOC			
240	12%	$1,000	$989,255
JOE			
240	12%	$1,324	$1,309,774

So Joe Average can do better than a doctor? That's what I am saying. If Doc could delay his desires and maybe stay married, he could be light-years ahead of Joe and most everyone else. It doesn't take $17,000 a month to live in most parts of the United States right now.

In the highly contrived examples above, let's say that Doc and Mrs. Doc will divorce—I am sure that the alimony and child support going to the Trophy Wife (his second ex-wife)—and Armando—will be much more than he is paying to Medical School Wife. Money is indifferent to who owns it. It doesn't matter if you drive a truck or are chief surgeon at the Mayo Clinic.

It is like an expanded example of Aesop's classic fable of the tortoise and the hare. The hare always thinks he can "make up time" (or in this case that he can always make more money).

While the tortoise makes regular faithful deposits to his wealth plan, the hare races from paycheck to paycheck, always thinking that he can earn more, all the while indulging his desires and ignoring the fundamentals of money. In the end, the hare is dependent on taxpayers to support him, while the tortoise hires the hare's children to tend his garden.

Here are Mrs. Joe's savings:

Number of Monthly Payments	Rate (Yield)	Monthly Investment	Future Value
240	12%	$500	$494,628

If the Rock of Gibraltar Fund worked as well for Mrs. Joe in roughly seven and one-half years (eighty-eight months) she would have enough to become Mr. and Mrs. Billy Bob's landlord.

Number of Monthly Payments	Rate (Yield)	Monthly Investment	Future Value
88	12%	$500	$70,000

Her $70,000 investment now brings in $700 a month plus the $500 from the doll dresses. With 12½ of the twenty years to retirement remaining, the new math with the same resolve could look like this:

Number of Monthly Payments	Rate (Yield)	Monthly Investment	Future Value
150 (12.5 years)	12%	$1,200	$413,811

Don't get too wrapped up in the math here or the imaginary Rock of Gibraltar Fund. And don't call me for their imaginary phone number. Grasp the concept. It is unlikely that you will earn 12 percent today on funds *others* manage. Don't lose sight of the important part: the discipline to make the monthly deposits. No matter if the savings rate is 3 percent—if you don't loyally make the principle deposits, you won't have the ready capital when opportunity knocks. We must have capital to capitalize.

> *Repeat after me, "Burn rate determines fate!"*

It is your burn rate, not your income, that will determine your fate. This fundamental is as sure as gravity and as certain as earthly death. Spending, more than earnings, is the problem for most Americans. If you redirect your income to take care of your future, after a time you can have your heart's desires from the earnings of your investments. Repeat after me, "Burn rate determines fate!" Make it your catchphrase, sing it in a song, and write a catchy commercial to run in your mind. It should be part of your financial liturgy. Here I mean by *liturgy* a customary repertoire of ideas, phrases, or observances.

Perhaps you wonder whether all this is worth it. Will you be able to muster the fiscal responsibility, the financial maturity to be successful? As Dr. Phil McGraw is fond of saying, "We don't do ten-minute cures here." I am talking ten or twenty years of continued and sustained effort. You may be able to answer that only by looking back at the last ten or twenty years. How are you doing so far? Do you wish to change? Be sure that your past is indicative of your future. Our natural proclivity is to lean toward the status quo. While we may acquire disease from germs or viruses in the air, from our own actions and those we associate with we acquire vice and the habits of the Consumerati. Success comes from long obedience in the right direction.

The soap opera *Days of Our Lives* has this opening: "Like grains of sand through the hourglass, so are the days of our lives." I have never seen the show, but I have heard the admonition clearly! Truly, the days of your life will slip through the hourglass. Ultimately you may see that mixing this common yet absolute movement of time together with proven fundamentals of money handling will give you an exceptional life.

Jim Rohn says, "With sight you see things—with insight you see answers to things." Though you cannot see the future, it is pretty predictable. It will be where your bundle of habits take you.

Lower your burn rate. Get control of emotional spending. Make some very important mature life choices. No matter the amount of your income, wealth can be obtained, or even maintained, only through the amount you *don't spend.*

> *No matter the amount of your income, wealth can be obtained, or even maintained, only through the amount you* don't spend.

The Parable of the Marbles

Suppose that marbles—yes, just regular old cat's-eye marbles were our currency of exchange instead of dollars. And at the end of each week, let's say that you get 10 marbles for your five days of work. You come home and put them in your bucket. You take a marble from the bucket to the grocer and get a few groceries you need, you take a few and pay the rent, and maybe you go to the chariot races. At the end of the week, all of the marbles are gone. You are living at 100 percent burn rate. No problem—each week, you get 10 new marbles. The process starts over again.

You see a new chariot you really want; it costs 300 marbles.

The friendly chariot dealer says that you may just pay 2 marbles a week for 150 weeks and then you will own the chariot outright. It's a no-marble-down deal! He also has a deal for 288 marbles for the same chariot that includes a 12-marble rebate. The catch is that you have to have all 288 marbles on the table at once. You agree to the 2-marbles-a-week deal. Presently, you find your bucket empties sooner; you miss your old chariot, the one without marble payments. Oh well, no chariot races this week and only 149 more marble payments to make.

Soon you get a raise. Now you make 13 marbles a week. The extra marbles are nice, but you find now you are making enough that the marble tax is beginning to take its toll. Between the accumulated marble payments for furniture, food, the bigger home, clothes to go with your big-marble lifestyle, and the marble tax, you find it difficult to live comfortably. You are certain that the marble tax is unfair—they should tax only the folks who earn the big shooter marbles. After all the taxes, counting state, local, and federal marble levies, you feel like you are losing your marbles.

If we train ourselves properly before we have a high debt-to-marble ratio, we would not lose our marbles. Suppose that, at a very young age, when you throw your 10 marbles into the bucket, you resolve to never take out more than 9 of the marbles for any expense—no matter what! So what would happen to your bucket eventually? Would it overflow? Say yes! Then you take that bucket of marbles and rent them, perhaps to the First Marblehead Savings Bank of Marblehead, your hometown. In case you didn't follow, money is like marbles. The *rent* on the marbles is the *interest* they pay you to use your marbles or your money. First Marblehead Savings then lends out your marbles, collects, say, 8 marbles a year for the use of 100 marbles, and pays 2 or 3 marbles to you for the rent.

You repeat the process, never taking more than 9 marbles of each 10 out of your bucket. After a few buckets of marbles have been deposited at the bank, perhaps you find a direct investment. Maybe you could earn 8 or 10 marbles per hundred or more if you took the risk and began to invest your marbles privately. It could be an extra house you rent out for 12 marbles a month. This would increase your income from 676 marbles a year to 820 marbles a year.

You may even find your marble tax lower from owning the investment rental—and marbles earned as rent are not subject to the marble security tax, which the 676 marbles earned from your employer are. Between you and your employer, you lose 15.7 percent of your marbles on this one tax. If you faithfully never take more than 9 of each 10 marbles out of your bucket to spend, eventually you can replace the 676-marble job income with passive marble income from investments, rental real estate, mortgage paper, mutual funds, or other investments. I know little about marble mutual funds. Some people tell me that they make a lot of marbles from them. I prefer an active investment where you can control a majority of the outcome.

Even once you replace the need for a job (most people just change to a more agreeable vocation), you must continue the 9-marbles-out-of-10 spending plan even with your passive marble investment income to grow even wealthier and shield against losses and inflation. A chariot that presently costs 300 marbles may cost 550 marbles by the time you retire.

Moral of the parable: Don't lose all of your marbles; hard work alone won't make us successful; we must accumulate capital and knowledge also.

Points to Ponder

- It is hard to see spending as a problem while all of your existing needs and many desires are being met.
- Debt early in life can set a pattern of nearly perpetual spending and borrowing that can lead to your financial ruin.
- Simply said, burn rate is all the money spent that does not increase your wealth. Burn rate is what is consumed and gone forever. Taxes account for a major part of your burn rate, together with food, shelter, and transportation.
- If you are now forty years old, every $100 monthly you burn (spend) knocks out $132,000 of potential retirement nest egg.
- Even if you feel that you can always make more money, you will run out of something else: time.
- Whether you are Joe Average or Dr. Lotta Bucks, your personal burn rate will determine your fate.

Chapter Four

Delayed Gratification: Don't Wait to Get It

The ten-second lesson: "Are we moral cowards or mathematical illiterates? Shouldn't we accept delayed gratification as a virtue and not a punishment? Using bad debt to take the waiting out of wanting eventually leaves you wanting."
—Jon Hanson

The lovely toy so fiercely sought hath lost its charm by being caught.
—Lord Byron

Perhaps the most damaging aspect of today's culture is short-term thinking. In America, we are anxious for everything—we want it now! The wisdom of the ages tells us to be anxious for nothing. Advertisers and popular culture heap the polite fiction "you can have it all" on us thousands of times daily, helping to create a "consumer entitlement mentality." We are moved from awe, to I'd like to have that, to I must have that, and finally to I am entitled to that! Where entitlements are perceived, neither common sense nor actual need is considered.

The clarion call of the Consumerati rings from mall to mall: "I want it all and I want it now!" The uninformed and the ignorant are always at the mercy of the merchants of the world. Herbert Spencer wrote, "The chief difference between the savage and civilized man is civilized man's ability to think and plan ahead for another day." Yet many of us choose to live like savages, never thinking of tomorrow. Cicero wrote, "Not to have a mania for buying things is to possess a revenue."

From the tattered slums to the gated communities in our most exclusive neighborhoods, we see the effects of good debt versus bad debt—our refusal to delay our immediate desires finds us ultimately with a fraction of what we could rightfully claim. Freedom lost, money spent, time not our own, golden opportunities missed—such are the memories of the Consumerati. Whether we are from the meanest streets in Detroit or the finest in Beverly Hills, time and money will show us to be fools or geniuses.

Vote for Me and I'll Set You Free!

Have you ever heard of the Delayed Gratification Party? No? If it did exist, by current standards only a small percentage of us would join or vote for it. Here is its platform: delayed gratification; spend less than you make; provide for your own future; put back more than you take; continue your own self-education; maintain personal responsibility and self-government. This would probably not be a very successful platform to run for political office on. It's enough to make a Libertarian blush. No, it does not sound like a political party platform at all, and it isn't.

The answer is not in political reform anyway. No vain vision of a utopian government will ever cure the ills of society. Only a change in the hearts of men and women can do that. The government can't straighten out your finances—it can't even straighten out its own. What Americans view as "poverty" would actually be great wealth in most parts of the world. Poverty, as we know it, is a lighter burden to bear than debt. Economist Thomas Sowell in an article on envy said, "Someone in his native India told best-selling author Dinesh D'Sousa that he wanted to see America because he wanted to see a country where poor people are fat. He was right. Americans in the lower income brackets are obese more often than those in the upper brackets."

> *Whether we are from the meanest streets in Detroit or the finest in Beverly Hills, time and money will show us to be fools or geniuses.*

Sowell continues, "Most Americans living below the official poverty line have air-conditioning, microwaves and VCRs. About half have a car or truck." So, then, let's ask ourselves what poverty is.

Two hundred years or more before Sowell, Ben Franklin wrote, "It is the eyes of others and not our own eyes which ruin us. If all the world were blind except myself I should not care for fine clothes or furniture." Today we could add cars, boats, starter mansions, and many, many other things. Thinking that we need to do as others do, many of us are afraid to stand alone. The problem is not new. We have more people with poor spending habits than we have poor people.

> We have more people with poor spending habits than we have poor people.

Have you ever picked up that new car or truck and then made a trip a wee bit out of your way so someone might be sure to see you driving your shiny new assemblage? I remember the afternoon I picked up the Jaguar that I discussed in Chapter 2 ("Emotional Hostage"). I drove to several friends' houses to show off the Jag, but no one was home. I remember thinking, Boy, it's no fun to have this great car and no one to see me driving it! I drove around until 11 PM and then went home—I could not find one person I knew to help me gratify my ego.

Had I learned the lessons of delayed gratification and been willing to act on them, I would have saved my money or at the very least invested it with greater discernment and never made such a foolish purchase. I robbed myself of feeling the internal gratification found only through wise decisions.

The Consumerati Just Want to Have Fun

What fun is it to look good if no one sees you? Robin Williams, speaking of an award for writing, once said, "Being a famous author is like being voted the best-dressed woman on radio." Williams's sardonic wit underlines the fact that many of us truly practice vanity to impress others—and gratification of our ego is dependent upon others looking at us.

During retirement, if money is tight, will it comfort you to recall how "prosperous" you *looked* in your Lexus with all of the right accessories that necessarily go along with being the typical

Lexus driver? Most Lexus drivers do not seem to suffer the common lives of the masses—at least not Lexus drivers in television commercials. I wrote in my journal recently a reflection of a few hours' television viewing (commercials mostly)—in jest of course: "I wonder if ugly people ever buy anything?" They are almost never represented in the commercials targeting the masses.

We derail the very success we seek when we step off the path to pretend that we have arrived. The inability of the Consumerati (pretenders) to delay gratification keeps the cash drawers of our merchants overflowing. The very essence of delayed gratification is to stay the course until we meet with success uncommon to those who cannot delay their desires.

While burn rate may be a mathematical and easily definable concept, the control of it is largely an emotional concept. The best ways to manage burn rate and delayed gratification are:

- Measurement—Some of us practice politically correct record keeping—we do not really want to know the truth. Continued deception is easiest if you do not have an accurate accounting.
- Control of your emotions—This means delayed gratification.
- A plan to follow—Continuous education is the key.
- Delaying allows accumulation—a key element of wealth building.

How unfair is life to inflict emotion at the beginning of a math problem? Delayed gratification is a math problem that is often distorted by emotions and desires distracting you from seeing a simple answer.

How unfair is life to inflict emotion at the beginning of a math problem?

I know of no way to avoid this problem, save for early training or later failure. This assumes that you learn from your failures. Old age may also teach you—

let's hope that you won't be too old to apply what you have learned. I think here of the eighty-year-old man who finally figured out the mysteries of women but no longer cared.

How you spend your money is a moral concept as well as a practical test of wisdom. I think most of our ill-conceived spending begins in these four broad areas, all variations of *Homo Consumerati:*

- Immature Consumerati
- Emotional Consumerati
- Selfish Consumerati
- Ignorant (by choice) Consumerati

Immature Consumerati. These are the people who do not see that their actions and how they live their lives (spend) have a large impact on their families and the world around them. This type of spendthrift does not grasp the basic concepts of money: that we must spend less than we make, that our ability to earn is not unlimited, that time is not on our side. The Immature Consumerati are usually selfish or ignorant of their actions. If a spendthrift grand jury were convened, perhaps the immature spendthrift would be charged with "depraved indifference" or "negligent spendicide." Immaturity is a tough problem because if you are truly immature, you probably don't know it. If someone points it out to you, it generally causes anger. A large part of being mature is admitting the areas where you are still immature. We all have them—we all have room and need to grow.

Emotional Consumerati. This is the area that gets most of us. Our senses get excited and we believe, at least for the time it takes to spend, that having "things" will make us happy. Many who follow this path find themselves with carefully furnished lives devoid of true happiness. The problem is then compounded if you have accumulated your "happiness" on credit. The Emotional Consumerati are very much controlled by what they are certain they "must have." They must live in the right neighborhood, have the right pets, drive the right cars, and feel that they are successful.

The Emotional Consumerati often gain a feeling of power, of being in control, when they spend money—even if it's borrowed money that allows them to make the purchase. The feeling is similar to the high from caffeine, alcohol, drugs, or gambling. Anything we do repeatedly that gives us pleasure begins to take control over us. Indiscriminate spending often becomes like a drug, requiring a higher dose each time for us to get the same feeling. Beware.

Selfish Consumerati. Their luxury sports car is more important than having the home paid for, the retirement plan set, or their kid's education funded. Selfish Consumerati believe that life is really all about them—they are me-o-centric. Their selfishness comes back to haunt them in old age when they discover that their once potential wealth has been spent on trinkets and worthless junk. The Selfish Consumerati are interested only in what immediately benefits them personally.

Ignorant Consumerati. This is the saddest type of them all. At least the other three have reasons. To a point, ignorance is like immaturity in that you may be unaware of it. The ignorance I am describing here is one that has been chosen. I know that I may speak freely here, for the truly ignorant will never pick up a book like this. The group I am speaking of know in their hearts that there is a better way yet choose

> *Hoffer is correct—a man or woman with an excuse is set for life.*

to continue in darkness. Author and speaker Larry Winget says, "If you don't know any better, you are ignorant. If you know better and continue to do destructive things, you are stupid."

We have a choice of whether to learn or not. To many this freedom of choice is more troubling than no choice at all. "For many people, an excuse is better than achievement," says Eric Hoffer, "because an achievement, no matter how great, leaves you having to prove yourself again in the future. But an excuse can last for life." Do you know anyone who has been talking for years about the job or opportunity that got away as *the* reason why he is not successful?

Sometimes the alleged grievance happened many years ago. Many blame the government, taxes, discrimination, big business, or anything that suits them as a fanciful excuse. Hoffer is correct—a man or woman with an excuse is set for life. Such people often excuse themselves from striving and accept whatever life gives them without too much effort and planning. When we have excuses ready for dispensing, it temporarily soothes the awful reality that we are where we are presently because of our own choices. It allows us to ignore that we failed to plan, that perhaps our whole philosophy of life is wrong. Many hate to admit they have followed the pied piper of consumerism to an unpleasant end.

By embracing excuses, many never even see that they could achieve a better life through wise handling of the limited resources they already have. The average twenty-first-century American family will handle more than $2.8 million over a forty-year period (based on 2002 figures; the actual amount will go up, adjusted for inflation). In seems ironic, given the amount of money we handle, that most people will end up broke and dependent on the government or others for their retirement. The concepts of *Good Debt, Bad Debt* do not discriminate against anyone. Earlier I said, "Money is no respecter of persons; it works equally for or against all who will give it employment." The sooner we take charge of our personal finances, the better off we will be in our inevitable and inescapable old age.

Two Roads

I monitor various news services, and I find the habits of the Consumerati are not unique to Americans. It seems the UK and Australia are in similar straits, as are many other countries. I even see a lot of articles on the evils of consumer debt from historically frugal Scotland. I did a lot of research on this early in developing *Good Debt, Bad Debt,* and no matter how far you go back in written history, man has always coveted what another man has. The Debt Devil and Madison Avenue depend on this. The emotional appeal was being used to separate men and women from their money long before the credit card industry came along. Perhaps it is faster now, but the pernicious effects are the same.

Are you destined to be a member of either the Consumerati or the Econowise? It would seem so. No one is perfect; we all have our Consumerati moments. The objective is to become more Econowise than Consumerati, more prudent than spendthrift. Unless you have built or bought your home without the aid of a loan, you must thank the members of the Econowise. All capital comes from the labor of the savers/investors of the Econowise. Labor comes in the form of brain work or back work. Capital comes from labor, and stored labor is capital: stocks, bonds, notes and mortgages, real estate, and cash savings.

While both the Consumerati and the Econowise labor and earn money, only the Econowise add to the pool of capital available to everyone. Without the Econowise, the Consumerati would have little capital to borrow. You may have capitalists and socialists, but you can never have socialists without the capitalists to start them out. You never hear of socialists starting or building something (with their own money). They need a host to survive, like a tick living off the blood (capital) of others. Socialists acquire "things" through political "reform" or force. Remember the words of the '70s philosopher Alvin Lee of the band Ten Years After in the song "I'd Love to Change the World": "Tax the rich, feed the poor, 'til there are rich no more." Can a government give you something it does not first take from you?

In our rush to appear successful or wealthy, we are deceived willingly to buy a boatload of fluff—and maybe even a boat on the installment plan! It is ironic that people will borrow money to make an *appearance* of wealth even though the payments for all of our toys, properly redirected, could lead us to *actual* wealth. With easy credit we begin to train an unnatural appetite that can lead us down the path to slavery. If you will delay gratification and begin to redirect your income to positive pursuits, eventually your wise money handling will allow you to afford the things you desire without pledging your future income to own them.

> *Debt that replaces debt—though perhaps on different terms—is nevertheless debt.*

I laughed aloud one day while I was in a bank making a deposit. The bank had a beautifully printed four-color poster showing a young couple and offering a $10,000 loan with the caption "Get out of debt! Only $99 a month." This was exceeded only by an e-mail from my phone company for DSL computer service with one of the benefits listed as "Free self-installation!" I told my wife that perhaps we should sign up now before they start charging us to let us install it ourselves.

Though the bank poster was a creation of an advertising agency, we can assume that the agency studied its target audience. Have we really descended to a level where borrowing more money is seen as getting out of debt? Debt that replaces debt—though perhaps on different terms—is nevertheless debt. Converting bad debt to a real estate loan does not make bad debt good debt. Borrowing to get out of debt makes all the sense of spending more at a "30 percent off sale" to save even more. Never mind the 70 percent outlay that accompanies the 30 percent imaginary savings. Don't allow yourself to be fooled by these semantic deceptions so common in today's advertising and media. You must take charge of how you sort and use the words that come to you. Separate the words from your emotion.

Cancer—Time to Be Serious

Suppose you had lung cancer and for treatment you were given the choice of two drugs. One drug would ease the pain but not cure the cancer. The other would cause some pain, maybe even a little more than you presently are experiencing, but would completely cure the cancer in a few years. Which drug would you opt for?

Is the best choice any different from what I am recommending here? Awareness, maturity, controlled burn rate, delayed gratification, careful record keeping, and a fiscally mature plan are the ingredients to blend into the apothecary jar for this medicine. Or you can opt, as many do, for a little debt and no planning to ease the pain but continue the financial cancer.

While no one can mix you the actual potion as I prescribe above, all of these ingredients are common and available for you to blend yourself. With public libraries, bookstores, the Internet, eBay, amazon.com, bn.com, and thousands of other resources, you would be hard pressed to convince me that you do not have the opportunity that each of us has. We are a population living intellectually malnourished lives in a country overflowing with free knowledge and information.

How Can I Make It Worse?

Some couples I have talked to refinance to lower their payments on consumer debt and then become unable to resist having all of their credit cards available again. They use them and soon find they are deeper in debt. They not only owe for the new and growing pile but also have added all of the former pile to secured debt on their personal home—much to the dismay of their bankruptcy attorney. This is a classic Consumerati move—make sure you are always heading uphill pulling a wagon full of debt.

The Consumerati are very concerned with keeping up appearances. They live in the sweet now (and now) and never consider the sweet by-and-by, as they buy and buy! They live in fear of others' opinions of their lives. Sadly, as the Consumerati continue to borrow and spend, the money they expend to appear wealthy could in a few years make them actually wealthy. People underestimate themselves. They have infinitely more resources than they think.

The Consumerati deceive themselves into thinking that "things" will make them happy. But what they find are only pleasures as shallow as the moment and despair as long as the payments.

The courage to join the Econowise, to be thrifty, and to practice a sensible economy is a moral choice requiring wisdom. That's why in this chapter's ten-second lesson I said, "Are we moral cowards or mathematical illiterates?" (I would assume that, once you are aware of the mathematical outcome of your poor spending habits, you will continue on that path only if you lack moral character or don't understand the math.)

There is another more common choice: you choose to deceive yourself, to tell yourself that you will take care of your future later. Later is sooner than you think. The ancestors of the haves and the have-nots are the dids and the did-nots, respectively. Without exception in matters of beginning saving or investment, sooner is better but *more* sooner is best.

When we decide to wait to begin our plan, rationalizing that we will start being thrifty and wise another day, we are really saying, "Just give me the leftovers of life." **Discipline delayed is discipline denied.** Compound interest needs time. The investments of youth are ever more fertile than the investments of the older person. The acquisition of good habits and a savings plan must begin as soon as the wet blanket of debt is lifted from you. A sixty-year-old has little more option than to pare down debt and arrange his financial affairs. He could well live to be ninety or more, so a financial plan is not futile—but oh, how much more powerful if he began at twenty or younger. While we wait to develop good habits, the poor habits become stronger and far less likely to ever be replaced. I gave a few examples of time and money for you to consider in Chapter 3 ("Burn Rate").

Pay as You Go

Statistically, only 3 to 5 percent of the population will retire without being at least somewhat dependent on others. The reason that people do not retire wealthy usually has little to do with the lack of income or monster salary, and has everything to do with their spending habits. Perhaps we should not follow the lead of the 95 percent that are heading for failure.

In *Architects of Fate*, Orison S. Marden relates the following anecdote: "The eccentric John Randolph once sprang from his seat in the House of Representatives, and exclaimed in his piercing voice, 'Mr. Speaker, *I have found it.*' And then in the stillness that followed this strange outburst, he added, 'I have found the Philosopher's Stone: *it is, pay as you go* [emphasis added].' "

What needs to be added is for one of his contemporaries to have said, "What if you can't always pay as you go?" Then the philosopher's answer could have been "Don't go! Sir, don't go!"

The "pay as you go" story is humorous to me, especially since it comes from a member of Congress. As Marden implies, unfortunately government can pass no law that will remedy the vice of living beyond one's means. If you can't pay as you go, stay home!

In the richest nation of the world, we find our hearts full of insatiable desires that keep our bank accounts empty. Hosea Ballou, the first president of Tufts College, said, "Real happiness is cheap enough, yet how dearly we pay for its counterfeit."

It ties to rule number 1 of economy, "Spend less than you make!"

> *What if the scarlet letter were D for debt and not A for adultery? If we all had to wear a symbol of our financial acuity on our chest, would it change how we handled our finances?*

The Scarlet Letter D Is for Debt

What if there were a stigma attached to being in debt for an accumulation of worthless items? In *The Scarlet Letter,* a woman accused of adultery is sentenced to wear a scarlet letter on her dress. What if the scarlet letter were D for *debt* and not A for *adultery?* If we all had to wear a symbol of our financial acuity on our chest, would it change how we handled our finances?

What are the rules for handling debt? In every chapter I have hinted at control of your emotions. A key point for most of us will be this control of emotions. Feelings precede actions.

In one of my many pages of notes I made for this book, I wrote, "I have a leash on my emotions." Then I added, "Some of us will need a log chain."

I agree with Ben Franklin's words, "It is the eyes of others and not our own eyes which ruin us." We live in fear of what the Joneses will say. Many retire with little or nothing to show for their years of toil except junk and worn-out trinkets. A wonderful life awaits those who rise above what others think—it is so simple, so genuinely sublime that many overlook it all of their lives. Thus you have another definition of the Consumerati: they consume all they have and mortgage their futures by borrowing all they can. They are left with little to show for it in the end.

Reality Math

Jimmy Napier taught me a mathematical truism you probably won't like: **Take your net worth, divide it by the number of years you have worked, and that is how much you are working for per year. This is your** *reality income.* Strive with me here for a moment. The key to delayed gratification and burn rate lies here: no matter if you make $100,000 a year, only what adds to your net worth is yours. How many folks do we talk to who are making more money than they ever dreamed of, yet at the end of the year or even after five or ten years they have little or nothing to show for it? Your burn rate controls your fate. I can't say it enough. It is a function of what you spend more than what you earn. If you have a net worth of $150,000 and have worked for twenty years, you are in fact working for $7,500 per year. The rest has been burned. I have a friend whose son and daughter-in-law make $156,000 a year collectively and have no assets other than a skinny equity in a highly leveraged house. In fact, if you count what was "borrowed" from Dad, Visa, and MasterCard, they spent $179,000 last year. They have been working for five years and have a net worth of probably $25,000 in their home before costs of selling. So could you accurately say that they are handling over $150,000 a year but working for $5,000 a year? Net worth equals $25,000 divided by 5 years of toil, which equals $5,000 per year. I'd like to think that this is an extreme example, but I have heard it over and over, usually from parents of high-income professionals. I am hoping that this example is so extreme that you will grasp the concept. Delayed gratification and your burn rate will determine your wealth more than income—even a very high income.

Points to Ponder

- The interesting thing about applying delayed gratification is that over time many of your wants will change. Recall Lord Byron's words, "The lovely toy so fiercely sought hath lost its charm by being caught."
- Compound interest is powerless to help your assets multiply if your investment capital is used for immediate wants.
- The opposite of delayed gratification is immediacy. You are falling into the trap of immediacy if you are spending money on appearing to be wealthy. The money many spend to appear wealthy could in time make them actually wealthy.
- The Consumerati deceive themselves into thinking that things will make them happy. But what they find are only pleasures as shallow as the moment and despair as long as the payments.
- Discipline delayed is discipline denied. Don't wait to apply delayed gratification; begin now. The inability to delay gratification is the death of every wealth-building program. In matters of saving and investing, sooner is better but even sooner is best.

Chapter Five
I Don't Know About My Past:
But My Future Is Spotless!

Hey, guys! Wait up!
This horse is heavy!

*The ten-second lesson: "Use your past as a reference library—
not a place to live!"*
—Jon Hanson

It's never too late to be what you might have been.
—George Eliot

I was cut from very average cloth. I heard the term *white trash*
more than a few times while growing up. The lesson to be learned
is that you should use your past as a reference—not as a place to

live. Many years that could be otherwise productive are often spent ruminating over perceived injustices. The choice is simple: will you use your past as a launch pad to be bitter or better?

The father says to the son, "I'm concerned about you being at the bottom of your class." The son replies, "Don't worry, Dad. They teach the same things at both ends." Within a classroom, this might be true. But within neighborhoods throughout America, the lessons can be very different.

I was born in Poverty, Illinois. We moved soon after that—probably at the urging of a landlord. My early childhood unfolded in Wenomoney, Wisconsin. I have fond memories of Wenomoney* and some I'd rather not recall. One of my fond memories was having "snow ice cream." At the time, I didn't know it was only a pan of snow, some vanilla extract, and a cup of white sugar beaten with an old mixer or spoon. To my sister and me, it was always a treat.

The Potato Incident

One of the times I'd rather not recall, though it's forever etched in my mind, is what I call the "potato story." I do not recall whether it was winter or summer (I was about five), but I remember going into the kitchen one day and finding my mom crying into the sink while she peeled potatoes. It was one of those old sinks with a side drain built in and a curtain around the bottom. I said, "Mommy, what's wrong?" And Mommy came unraveled. She sobbed, "We're broke! Your dad's out of work, we are lucky to have the electric on, the rent is due, and on top of all that I had to go next door to borrow four potatoes just to feed us!" And she didn't mean a side dish. It was a four-

---

* Wenomoney, Wisconsin, is a composite of Menomonie, Hershey, Spring Valley, and Wilson, all around Dunn County, Wisconsin.

person, four-potato meal. The more she vented her grief, the harder she wept. It was gut wrenching for me.

I was only a child and had never seen this type of thing role-played on *Oprah* with Dr. Phil. I didn't know what to do. It's been said, "In the old days people lived quiet lives of desperation. Today they go on national talk shows." That day in the kitchen I think we both just sat on the floor and cried ourselves out. My five-year-old subconscious filed away the incident and, in the back of my mind, I have worked in part to not ever return to four-person, four-potato meals. This one incident has been a large motivating factor in my life.

Soon after the potato incident, my family moved to Hardscrabble, Ohio, to take care of my mother's mother (read: free rent). I don't recall what Dad did at the time, but for most of my memories, he was a self-employed carpenter. The only place around Hardscrabble to get regular work was at the pottery plant in Crooksville, Ohio, and no one we knew worked there.

Hardscrabble was about the size of Wenomoney—three saloons and a jot 'em down store. In Hardscrabble, mediocrity was something you aspired to. In retrospect, the view from Hardscrabble, Ohio, was very different than from Suburbia, USA.

School was fun and I made a few friends whom we would soon leave. I don't recall how long we stayed in Hardscrabble. I know that we stayed until they carried Grandma out in a bag.

The one thing I remember after Grandma died is that Mom got an old quilt and a Singer pedal sewing machine as her inheritance. Her older brother and his wife, the ones with the "good" jobs, got the house and figured it was time for the trash to move on. So we did.

My uncle then installed indoor plumbing and put really nice white aluminum siding on the house. After the house was remodeled, they rented it to what seemed like a really nice family whom I would see from a distance when forced to go to those great family reunions in Hardscrabble. I really never missed Hardscrabble, probably because even as a six- or seven-year-old, I felt Grandma got a raw deal. The house could have been fixed up for Grandma. It always seemed to me that Mom's sisters and brothers looked down at us. Actually, it didn't matter. We took what we were given and had lived rent-free for a while by taking care of Grandma.

November 22, 1963

After they planted Grandma (in the cemetery), we moved to Kirkersville, Ohio. I drove by our old Kirkersville house a few months ago. Of course, it looked a lot smaller than I remembered. It was yet another rental house with still another landlord (I think the landlord lived next door). This one had an outhouse too, but also indoor plumbing!

This is where we were living when President Kennedy was assassinated. I remember hearing the announcement over the scratchy PA system in school that President Kennedy had been shot. My teacher was sobbing. School let out right after the announcement. It was November 22, 1963. I had just turned seven years old. My mom cried for several days.

It seemed to me that the black-and-white TV had only the Kennedy funeral and talking heads for days. I vaguely remember the scene with John-John saluting his father's casket as it went by. I just wanted it all to be over. I missed Captain Kangaroo, Mr. Green Jeans, and Tom Terrific.

Bright Lights, Big City—Is the Door Locked?

From Kirkersville we moved to the big city of Columbus and lived in a neighborhood that people most often referred to by saying, "Oh my, do you feel safe there?" We lived on the corner of Gloom Alley and No Future Street. A few blocks from our twin single dwelling, Interstate 70 was being constructed. Some of the bridge support columns were poured near our home as construction progressed. As you may have already guessed, freeway bridge abutments are hallmarks of finer neighborhoods.

The rent was $52.50 a month. I remember this because $52.50 was evidently a lot of money. It was a frequent topic of discussion for Mom and Dad in those days. There was always talk of money at home, but mostly about the *lack* of money—not how to save, invest, or earn more.

Our landlord's name was Duke. He had purchased a new home in Sun Valley in Madison Township. I'm sure my dad envied Duke. I was over at their new house a lot while my Dad helped Duke add a few things to the place. I'm still not sure if Dad was working off rent or being paid.

Poor People Have Poor Spending Habits

While we were paying the $52.50 a month, the thought of buying a house became a major topic for discussion. Nevertheless, a $600 color TV showed up before we ever got a house. We were the envy of the neighborhood—but consider the neighborhood. In 1966, color TV was rare. Many of the shows were still in black and white, but you could always look forward to *The Wonderful World of Disney* on Sunday evening.

The same $600 we squandered on the color TV could have gotten us out of the slums! Of course, I didn't think of that until years and years later. I never had any conversation with my parents regarding money, other than could I have a dime for a sixteen-ounce bottle of Frosty root beer or perhaps a Dilly Bar.

Years later I marveled at how the $600 squandered for the color TV was more than Duke had put down on his 1,100–square-foot mansion. And we are talking 1,100 feet all on one floor! His down payment for the FHA loan would have been 3 percent of $12,900. That comes to $387 for those of you in Hardscrabble.

> *Nearly uniform in the soul of the poor is that they'll do something stupid with their money if they are blessed to receive some now and then.*

Nearly uniform in the soul of the poor is that they'll do something stupid with their money if they are blessed to receive some now and then. I have repeated this unwise asset allocation many times in my life. Bad habit programming is hard to delete from your personal operating system.

Got a Light?

At the time, 1966, I didn't know what a pack of cigarettes cost, but between Mom and Dad, it took eight packs a day to support their habit. If we assume fifty cents a pack as a figure, this means about $1,400 a year was going up in smoke—which just coincidentally is about 15 percent of the total value of the double dwelling we were living in. It is also about three and a half times the down payment on Duke's 1,100–square-foot ranch in the suburbs. If we assume that the twin dwelling brought in $105 a month in income and expenses were 25 percent of the gross income, the value of the double would have been, say, $9,450.* Thus the money from seven years of cigarettes exceeds the total cost of the two-family dwelling. Please remember that these housing values are from 1966. But the lessons remain the same.

* This value would assume a 10 percent yield for the owner of the twin-single dwelling. The $945 net income per year is divided by 0.10 for a value of $9,450 (see "Up in Smoke," Chapter 5 notes, on www.gooddebt.com).

Naturally, at age nine, I didn't know all of this. I loved my family and believed that we were victims of circumstances far beyond our control. I later learned that entire political parties have been built on this be-a-victim philosophy. I imagined that some people just had it made—maybe they were lucky. Imagine Duke saving, buying properties (our home and others), and then reinvesting the proceeds. Yes, he was just, well, lucky. And he didn't smoke—so many unfair advantages.

Well, We're Moving On Up—to the Far Eastside

In 1966, a few people were beaten and shot near Gloom Alley. Walter Cronkite was on the news nightly talking about riots and racial unrest. My dad decided to buy a house in Reynolds- burg, Ohio. It was not a solution to race problems, but at least we were out of the direct line of fire. I remember Dad saying that he got shot at enough in the Philippines during World War II.

We bought the worst house avail- able in Reynoldsburg, which we could barely afford. We weren't ex- actly the Jeffersons, but being one of the poorest kids in Reynoldsburg, Ohio, seemed a grand elevation from where we were before. Dad eu- phemistically called this $8,500 hovel a *fixer-upper*. But it quickly became a *"never-doner."* To this day it is still a dump. Most every town has "the poor part," and we were comfortably ensconced in the slums of Reynoldsburg. Ah, life was good.

> *Dad euphemistically called this $8,500 hovel a fixer-upper. But it quickly became a "never-doner."*

I think here of the preacher who says, "I'd rather have a shack in Heaven than a mansion on Broadway." Reynoldsburg, though far from Heaven, was the first place we lived where I actually felt safe.

In Reynoldsburg it quickly became apparent to me that there were very different classes of people. It was also apparent that we were in the part that made up the lower end of the scale. After all, some of the townsfolk lived in $25,000 houses and never wanted for food or clothing. It is doubtful that any had ever seen their mother weep over a kitchen sink while peeling four borrowed potatoes. The potato incident had made a watermark on my mind; I could see through it, but it was always there. I vowed to myself privately, I would never have to live like this again; my kids would have food and shelter—a better life. This was actually one positive aspect of growing up in intermittent poverty. It provided kind of a negative goal-setting direction for me.

Reynoldsburg soon became a daily reminder of just how poor we were. I remember going to the A&P with my mom and getting a nine-cent ham bone to float in the beans for the flavor. Can you imagine nine cents? Sometimes the butcher would just give it to us and wave us on with a dismissive swipe of his hand. That actually hurt worse than just paying the lousy nine cents. Perhaps this was the butcher's version of charity. It didn't feel like charity to me though. I felt like we were being banished from the table and thrown a scrap.

> *The potato incident had made a watermark on my mind; I could see through it, but it was always there.*

I don't believe that we were ever in danger of starving. It just seemed to be a constant struggle for my parents to keep food on the table. There was a steady diet of navy beans, corn bread, oatmeal, cornmeal mush, and, in prosperous times, maybe spaghetti. While the food situation seemed a little better in Reynoldsburg, the clothing situation became worse.

Certainly, if your past has many events where lack of money is the central focus, then how you "use" these events as you recall them will affect your philosophy of money. We like to think that the past doesn't matter, but so long as it is a glowing ember, it probably does. For me, it altered my ability to delay gratification. I was always eager to rush ahead, trying to outpace my white trash past.

Early Vocational School

Things were going pretty well in Reynoldsburg. Occasionally Dad would come by the school and take me to work with him. I carried tools and cut and hammered trim (on $40,000 houses, no less). One of our big jobs was putting oak trim in Thurber Towers in Columbus. I was out of school a lot during that job. My job was to slide along on the floor and drill holes in the baseboard with a finish nail in an electric drill. The nail didn't last too long and you needed only to touch it once before it cooled down and you'd never do that again. In early 1968, I was probably the best eleven-year-old trim carpenter in Ohio.

> *I was always eager to rush ahead, trying to outpace my white trash past.*

Everything Changes

One Friday night in May, Dad and I got the truck all loaded, ready to head out early in the morning for a remodeling job. I awoke Saturday morning, fearing that I had overslept and Dad had decided to leave without me. I ran downstairs to find my mom weeping on the couch. She had a look of profound grief, a look I had not seen since Wenomoney, Wisconsin, and the potatoes.

Then, out of the bedroom, gliding silently through the kitchen and the living room, past Mom and me, went the firemen matter-of-factly rolling a stretcher right past us with Dad's body covered with a white sheet. They put him into the ambulance and drove away—no lights, no sound, no Dad.

My dad died May 25, 1968. Martin Luther King had been assassinated just a month before. I think it rained for five days straight. My mom's people from Hardscrabble came up to advise us but not help in any way, financially or spiritually. My dad's oldest brother sent the money to fly Dad's body back to Wenomoney for burial. I don't remember how we got to Wenomoney, but everyone was kind. After about a week of sympathy and lots of good food, we returned to Reynoldsburg with our gullets full and our hearts heavy with doubt. Though I was only eleven, I knew the prospects for a better life had just taken a big nosedive.

Things were tough. Being eleven, I decided that I could get a paper route. I did and soon I had two early-morning *Citizen Journal* paper routes, making about $20 a week. Now $20 a week to a kid was big money in 1968, and soon I'd be twelve.

I was able to buy all my own clothes, which I did regularly. I had the popular Adidas tennis shoes and *store-bought* pants that fit. I even had a real barber "style" my hair instead of mom buzzing it or cutting around a bowl for the Beatles look.

Buck

Soon after my Dad had passed away, I met Mr. A. C. Bennett. Everyone who frequents his auto repair shop knows him just as

"Buck." You might think that a garage is a lousy place for an eleven-year-old to hang out. At times it probably was. But the location was good, being just a block or less from home, and the benefits were decent.

By observing Buck, I learned how to work on cars and how to talk to people and interact in a selling situation. More than that, though, Buck gave me a father figure to look up to and advise me. He was just as tough on the guys that hung out at his shop as he was on his own sons. If you had sufficient fortitude to survive the physical lessons, together with the verbal abuse dispensed and the constant negative character references, you could actually learn a trade. You could even learn the trade for free, if you don't consider the abuse to be a cost.

The best thing about Buck was, and still is, his unchanging set of standards. You knew that he was going to be tough on you, but you knew that he was going to be fair. And you knew that if you called him, he would come and get you or help resolve whatever the problem was. There was an unwritten rule— if he needed your help, you were expected to be there. That could mean helping to pump the brakes or push a car.

Sometimes I'd sweep the floor. Later, when I was older, I'd follow him to a customer's house to drop off a car and give him a ride back to the shop. His son David took over the shop years ago, but Buck still comes in almost every day to answer the phones and generally terrorize the uninitiated.

I talked over all my big decisions with Buck. "Hammerhead" was one of the more affectionate terms he used when speaking to me. When I was younger and an adult would try to push me around, I'd talk to Buck. The few times I had a serious issue, Buck helped me find an attorney. When I bought my first house or my first twenty or thirty cars (a little side business I had), or considered a new job, Buck was my adviser.

Watching Buck, I learned how to open up and talk with people. I imitated his mannerisms and jokes, and caught his values. I learned that the relationships he built with people over the years benefited him time and time again. Integrity and consistency are Buck's standards. Though he ran a little garage, he was really quite a salesman. I watched him buy and sell cars. I used all of his tools and heated his garage to fix up my old cars and sell them. He helped me with most of the things I could have expected a dad to do.

I never realized, until Buck's ninetieth birthday party on October 26, 2001, that besides the garage, Buck had a sort of "fathering" service. Many of the old gang and plenty of lifelong customers were there. How many people do you know who would go to a party to honor their mechanic? When I looked around the hundred or so people, there were a lot of familiar faces. Mike, Rick, Bruce, and Jerry were some of the guys who had experiences similar to mine.

My son, A. C., is named after Mr. A. C. Bennett. My son will never know the deprivation that "Grandpa Buck" knew or even the lesser pain I knew. What I want him to take from Grandpa Buck is his integrity, wit, tenacity, and long life—all the qualities I have tried to emulate from years of watching Buck. I often introduce Buck by saying, "This is my adopted dad." The statement is quite succinct. He never adopted me; I adopted him. Like a stray cat, I showed up at his garage thirty-four years ago and never really left.

Let's Move Again

In 1972, we moved to a government-assisted project (People Stacker Apartment Houses, 228 of them on fourteen acres or so) in Madison Township. Mom sold the house and I don't know if we made a penny on it. If we did, it was not evident in anything that affected me. Within a year, I was sixteen and driving, buying, and selling cars. I got my own apartment in Whitehall, Ohio, a small town between Reynoldsburg and Columbus.

Kroger Daze

I started working for Kroger Grocery Stores in August 1973 and quit school. I left school when I discovered that I was making more than my record-keeping teacher. If you think that I was surprised, he was nauseated. My teacher gave me some really bad advice: quit; you don't need this.

I spent nine years at Kroger and for the times, the pay was decent. The last few years, my attitude was pretty bad. I was looking for a way out. I remember a fellow at our store we'll just call Oscar Loser—that's pretty generic. He worked in one of the small departments and always had his pants where you could see—well, you might think he was a plumber. He had a terrible attitude. He was tired, grumpy, and generally unpleasant. He was Homer Simpson before Homer was a cartoon.

I went into the break room one day and Oscar was sitting there alone. He had an uncanny ability to repel a crowd quickly. Going into management with Kroger Company had been on my mind for several weeks.

I asked Oscar, just out of the blue, how old he was. I assumed he was fifty-five or more, since he could barely walk, his back and joints were broken down from carrying heavy boxes, and in general he looked terrible. He said he was thirty-three. I must have looked shocked. He said, "How old did you think I was?" It was a trap, like being asked to guess a woman's weight and you foolishly say a number. I avoided the answer.

Just then his family walked in. I had never seen them before. His wife was almost as big as his huge fifteen-year-old stepson. They argued for a while, exchanged a few unpleasantries, got some cash from Oscar, and were on their way.

As the stress in the break room eased, I asked Oscar what he thought his future with the company was. He said he hoped to just survive for five more years. I didn't know where he would be going in five years. He was broke and his domestic arrangement would make sure that was permanent. In retrospect, I now understand Oscar's behavior. If you count on your family to be your source of inspiration, we can safely assume that Oscar was near death in the inspiration department.

Oscar was the type of guy who could make conservatives reconsider their stance on assisted suicide or mercy killing. Apparently Oscar thought that he could retire after twenty years at Kroger. The catch was that you actually had to be fifty-five, not just have the mileage of a fifty-five-year-old. I watched Oscar light up another cigarette as I slowly backed out of the break room, fearing I might catch whatever Oscar had.

I didn't really have my heart in going into management anyway, but Oscar iced the deal. He was at best a reverse recruiting program for Kroger. After fifteen years, he was a bitter, broken man. Mom was right—no one is totally worthless. Anyone can at least be a good bad example.

I thought about Oscar a lot right after that, deciding that if in only ten years I would look like him and, worse, sound like him—or, God forbid, have his life—I had to get out of there. Oscar was almost bearable by himself. But when I considered the totality of his life and the direction it was leading him, it helped make my decision. I wanted out. I read and studied everything I could on positive thinking, sales, getting rich, and real estate.

Maybe Six Hours of College Will Help

Growing increasingly tired of being a Kroger automaton, I sat for a GED, passed it, and started college at Franklin University.

I have always thought that I would dedicate a book to my English teacher at Franklin. During a remedial English class, we were asked to write a few paragraphs on something we really liked. I wrote about my 1977 Chevrolet Caprice. Ms. Marcia Hollbrook (I think that's her name) marked the paper up and returned it to me. Luckily she had used a soft #2 red pencil because the paper had so many marks that otherwise you couldn't have seen the original writing.

After class, I went up to discuss the paper with Ms. Hollbrook. However poor a writer, I was nevertheless pragmatic. I simply desired to be better—to learn. As we talked, she seemed quite nice, and I mentioned that someday I'd like to write how-to books. She instantly fell over laughing and slapping the desk. I stood stoically and motionless, until she finally sensed that I was serious. She thought it quite inconceivable that I really meant it! She recovered by saying something nebulous like "Well, it's going to take a lot of work." So Ms. Hollbrook, thank you for at least not advising me to take six weeks off from writing, then quit. It has taken a lot of work. Being a consummate late-learner and, more importantly, having the *love* of learning and especially reading have made all the difference.

Please note I did finally finish college thirteen years later, in 1994. I graduated *summa cum barely* from the University of the State of New York, at Albany.

So What?

So what? Jon, what does all of this sad discourse about your past have to do with anything? The simple, profound point is that your environment really does affect your life. Wow, there's a news flash! You mean, if I'm born in one of those good neighborhoods, I'll have a better life than if I am raised in Hardscrabble? Well maybe, *perhaps only initially*. If you are able to understand the lessons you picked up from your past, you may do very well, even if you are a boy or girl from Hardscrabble.

> *"You are not born a winner or a loser, you are born a chooser."*

Conversely, we have all seen those who seemingly have every advantage but are unable to become wealthy, or dribble away wealth that was given to them.

What do we learn from the above? The ten-second lesson is to use your past as a reference library—not a place to live. My book-marketing mentor Mark Victor Hansen says, "You are not born a winner or a loser, you are born a chooser." You may operate with the mindset of a resident of Hardscrabble or the mindset of a Park Avenue blue blood. Let's see what we can check out of the ole library of the past. It took me thirty years to even write or discuss the events of this chapter.

I wrote this chapter sequentially, like a reporter. What you may not glean from the chapter is that I had and still have a profound love for my mom and dad. My dad was Eldon Edward Hanson; my mom was Beverly Sue Hanson. From my mom I get any drive and tenacity and dry humor I have. From my dad I get all of my creativity and problem-solving skills.

Over the past thirty-five years, the real growth in my life came from the foundation laid down by my dad and then built upon by the four or five men who affected me most throughout the years. In addition to these men, I've found role models through constant reading. Few men have affected my life more than my posthumous mentor, Orison Swett Marden. Though Marden died thirty-two years before my birth, I feel connected to him through his writing. He began writing at age forty-six and before his death in 1924 wrote over seventy books. If you have an open and curious mind, finding good father (or mother) figures who will teach you sound financial habits is not that hard. We are commanded to "honor our mother and father," yet are meanwhile also advised, "There is wisdom in many counselors."

Bitter or Better? Grasping a Useful Perspective

If you find yourself dealing with the loss of a loved one (I can tell you from experience), you are at a crossroad. Eschewing Robert Frost's advice in "The Road Not Taken," "Two roads diverged in the woods and I . . ."—well, I took the one most traveled. It would be a great story if I told you that I wasn't bitter for almost thirty years about losing my dad, but I was. Not only will bitterness hurt you financially from the distraction alone, it is hard on you both mentally and physically. I know a little about bitterness—the sooner you can dump it, the better off you will be financially and personally.

It was only a few years ago, while writing a eulogy for a four-year-old boy who had died of brain cancer, that I began to get a useful perspective on my past. I wanted the family and friends not to be bitter about their loss. It's amazing how often we wish for others what we won't do for ourselves. In Michael's eulogy I penned the words "*Will you use this event* [Michael's death] *to become bitter or better?*" I then realized that I had used my dad's death to become bitter—not outwardly and obviously, but there was a subtle undercurrent of bitterness. If my mind were a computer, this thought would be like an annoying pop-up window reading, "It's not fair," over and over again. This undercurrent was not enough to kill but just enough to slow growth and happiness. I accepted that the best thing for me to do was to learn from the past and move on. I am certain that I benefited more from organizing the notes for the eulogy than the family and friends did from hearing it.

The choice we have when faced with life's adversities is always to become bitter or better. Bitter seems the most reasonable and economical choice in the beginning. Yet to become better is the more profitable route in the long term. Will we drag the past along or leave it in the reference library? Will we learn the lessons of life or repeat over and over the same mistakes? Perhaps we are unaware that the game is afoot! This is your life, not a test run. Change is within the grasp of everyone.

It's Just Not Fair!

It's easy, though disheartening, to live in a world where you imagine that "fairness" is a uniform or even universal concept. Much of what is demanded in the world under the guise of fairness or tolerance is designed to be field leveling rather than uplifting. Jim Rohn says, "There are two ways to have the tallest building in town—build the tallest building, or tear down everyone else's!" Sometimes it's easier to indulge in pity, envy, and jealousy than to take a realistic inventory of our actual efforts. It will always be easier to support a "cause" or vote for someone who promises to "make things better" than to actually apply personal effort to make things better for yourself.

> *If my mind were a computer, this thought would be like an annoying pop-up window reading, "It's not fair," over and over again.*

Can government give to you anything it first does not take from you? In the end we must still strap on the boots and begin the climb. Years ago, I heard a TV comedian say, "It's a long, hard climb to the middle." Laugh, but do climb to the middle. It's on the way to the top and it's so much nicer than the bottom.

Points to Ponder

- What have you learned from your past? Does your past affect how you spend money? I learned early on that if you have money, spend it! No one around me modeled delayed gratification, so in the early years I didn't see it as important.
- Your past can stifle your growth or motivate you to do even more. Remember, you always have a choice: will you learn to be bitter or better?
- If you choose bitter, be aware that you may kill your ultimate plan by playing the revenge game: "I'll show them." Or, as one wit said, "Many spend their time and money buying things we don't need, to impress people we don't like." (See Chapter 2, "Emotional Hostage").
- Can you think of something that pulls the past into your present and future and keeps on affecting it? Give up? Debt. Remember, the past is the past unless you still owe for it.
- "He who controls the past commands the future. He who commands the future conquers the past," as George Orwell said.

Chapter Six
What If You Live?
Make Work a Stage of Life—
Not a Life Sentence

I sure wish your dad had spent our extra $125 a month
on life insurance instead of enhanced cable TV.

*The ten-second lesson: "I always thought that success was in
secrets I could learn. Near halftime in life, I find that financial success is a function of simple math and delayed gratification. There is dangerous ground between knowing and
doing—the great purgatory of inaction. It is here where
dreams die, life becomes ordinary, and we train ourselves to
accept far less than our potential by always seeking but never
coming to an understanding that life is as much doing as
thinking."*
—Jon Hanson

I remember thirty. Old enough to have been there, young enough to still get there, yet optimistic enough to wait.

—Jon Hanson

Twenty to life! That's the average sentence for a working American. Many will serve thirty to fifty years. Some choose to do hard time. Others think they have no choice. Remember the movie *Cool Hand Luke*? Paul Newman kept mumbling, "Gotta get my mind right, gotta get my mind right, boss!" Luke had a problem with authority. The authority we have been addressing throughout *Good Debt, Bad Debt* is the fundamental laws of money. The fundamentals of good and bad debt we reviewed in the first five chapters are your boss and your warden. They hold your keys to earthly freedom. This is true even if, like Luke, you don't take kindly to the idea. If you are not prudent, your twenty-year sentence can be increased, perhaps even to a life sentence.

Unless you were born wealthy, to retire comfortably you will serve a period of financial sacrifice. The well-trained mind sees this time period as a blessing and not a sacrifice. The earlier you start, the less severe the pain and the shorter the sacrifice. Success in retirement comes more from starting and sticking to a plan than from the actual investment. Almost every child knows that without a beginning, there is no middle and no end.

Are You in Jeopardy?

"Let's play Jeopardy! Alex, I'll take 'Good Timing' for $1,000!"

Alex replies, "The answer is 'Sooner is better, but more sooner is best.' "

Quick! Buzz in and say, "When should you start a retirement fund?"

"That's right!" says Alex. "You now have control of the board! Where do you want to go?"

In real life, if you wish control of the board (your financial life), start sooner on your investment plan, not later. Recall the question of the Econowise. At the beginning of every spending situation, they ask, "Does this take me nearer or farther away from my goals?"

> *Almost every child knows that without a beginning, there is no middle and no end.*

Most people put off thinking about retirement because they know that they won't like the answers to the questions they know they must ask. Rather than face these questions as mature men and women, sometimes they find it easier to develop what Jim Rohn once described as "happy hope." Mr. Rohn (I paraphrase here) described this as a man in his midforties who has done nothing to provide for his future, but merrily whistles along as if everything is grand. Can anything be worse than suddenly waking up at fifty years of age and finding that all you have is a rented life, that you own virtually nothing of value or consequence?

But I Have a Positive Mental Attitude (PMA)

Positive thinking is good, but not positively *deluded* thinking. I refer to these deluded types as afflicted with positive thinking, but not infected with a purpose, process, and plan. Afflicted with positive thinking? Can something *good* actually be *bad?* Yes, especially when it is only half applied. A college education is good, but if you never leave the house, of what use is it? Many lack the chutzpah to get things moving; the reality of moving a plan from concept to actualization can be daunting.

An insurance salesman named Ben said to me recently, "When I mentioned life insurance to a client the other day, he said, 'I don't need any, I'm with Jesus Christ Mutual.' " I told my friend, "Yes, that's an excellent company, but I think your prospect is confusing *assurance* with *insurance*. This fellow may be ready to leave this world, as he has blessed assurance, but it does nothing for his family, which in other parts of the Bible he is commanded to provide for." Assurance for Ben's prospect has to do with God's promise to him as a believer.

Assurance for our purposes has to do with the guarantee of a specific outcome if you follow the steps and start soon enough. For this assurance, you rely on math, compounding (time to grow), discipline, deferral, and discernment in selection of investments. Just as in assurance of salvation, for financial assurance you must take all of the steps. A quick affirmation and a prayer won't get you there.

Two-thirds of Americans dream of retirement, while only one-third actually take steps to move in that direction. Some rely on happy hope ("Everything will work out just fine," or "I have faith"). Faith without work and planning to back it up is just another form of delusion. Other people cite too little income to begin saving ("I'm young. I have plenty of time," or "It's too complicated"). We must keep in mind that the traits of the Econowise and, sadly, the Consumerati are sticky and elastic, and they scale to make you more of one or the other. The odds are that you will become more of what you already are. Our chances for success are better with a simple system that we always follow rather than a complex plan that we sometimes follow.

John Bogle, founder of the Vanguard Mutual Funds, says, "Simplicity gives us the power to do less of what doesn't matter— and gives us the power to do more of what does matter." Limiting options sounds like the wrong advice, doesn't it? Yet most would agree that picking the right option and sticking with it is a good limitation. I don't mean limiting your investment choices. I mean limiting your system to a simple process you can understand and stick to. How simple? Monthly, weekly, or biweekly, consider each deposit you make as a tank of oxygen that will last only until the next pay period. Without this tank of oxygen, your retirement plan could suffocate.

Through experience or study of great men and women, we find that sticking to the fundamentals of money handling will lead us to success. There is no such thing as a new fundamental. You may be as creative in the application of fundamentals as you wish—but if you violate their basic laws, you will fall short of your goals. If we violate the rules, we will not be paroled.

Thrift is the great educator. To apply thrift to your life, you must plan—you must have a written program to follow. Without such a plan, life is very inefficient and costly. To apply thrift is to understand timing and value. Thrift assumes forethought and careful reasoning. A large income is not necessarily an indicator of wealth. An income of almost any size strained through well-trained habits in time will create wealth.

Et Tu, Jonny?

It is one thing to admit to your financial shortcomings, yet quite another to escape the consequences.

I will always cherish my initial misconceptions of life. Given the vantage point of middle age and partially healed wounds, I see that many share these same misconceptions. Success looks easy when we are young. Life seems simple until you have lived a bit of it—and life can be simple, depending on the choices we make. We may live with the quaintness of what we choose to believe or the reality of what actually is.

I have found that it is one thing to admit to your financial shortcomings, yet quite another to escape the consequences. Certainly, our youth is the best time to develop a financial plan and follow it. If youth has passed you by, take the next best time—now.

Irony and the Obvious

The irony of youth is that while as a group young people could benefit the most from a wise program, they are the most unlikely to pursue one. It takes genuine maturity to become sophisticated and humble enough to believe in a simple system. Our egos would rather we live thinking that we accomplish great things by our own might or cleverness—not that success in life is by adherence to time-honored values. Perhaps we feel cheated or at least embarrassed when, after a long struggle, we find out how simple things really are.

Life presents us with many techniques but few fundamentals; it is easy to overlook the truly valuable among the many choices. The desire to think that we know something few others know causes many of us to overlook obvious truths. For me, real estate has always buoyed my portfolio. One of my big regrets is finding how simple it would have been to create a larger liquid portfolio to go along with it. Discipline, deferral, and discernment applied early in life can make a dramatic difference.

You Are Probably Closer Than You Think

Practical thrift, the right ordering of your finances, the practice of delayed gratification, and monitoring and control of your burn rate may be all that is separating you from the financial life you desire. Have you ever looked back on a five- or ten-year period and said, "If I could have concentrated on A, instead of B,

I would be at C." Sadly, I have. Your burn rate will determine your fate. Spending determines your ending.

Eventually we find that money is no respecter of persons—it works equally for or against all. Money does not care if you are famous, a highly paid professional, or the dishwasher at Waffle House. The fundamentals of money and debt do not discriminate. Money will perform equally well for all who will give it employment. A young person who begins to automate deposits into an investment monthly, biweekly, or weekly will end up with wealth far exceeding that of the average American.

Don't Wait, Automate

Make the decision in advance to get started on retirement savings. If you do not have the skills to direct-invest (meaning that you pick the investment), you can at least muster the ability to set up an automatic withdrawal from your paycheck or checking account each month to purchase shares of a mutual fund or bond fund. Begin today. If you are computer-savvy, you can set up a regular investment account or Roth IRA online and begin electronic withdrawals from your checking account or maybe even directly from your paycheck to fund it. If you are not computer-literate, most of the funds have 1-800 phone numbers.

> *It bears repeating: you must have capital to capitalize when opportunities arise.*

I will agree that it is easier for a W-2 wage-earning person than a self-employed person to automate savings and investments, but I do have self-employed friends who use the technique to make deposits from their checking accounts.

When I was a regular employee at Kroger, I had a stock purchase deduction, and a large portion of my weekly check went directly to the credit union. Looking back, I saved about 14 percent of my income at the time. It bears repeating: you must have capital to capitalize when opportunities arise.

Self-Taxation

Some argue that taxes are too high. I agree, yet we must accept that they are what they are. I recall reading about Ben Franklin saying to tax protestors, "The amount you tax yourself with drink and other vice far exceeds the British levies. The cost of one vice can support two children." I think old Ben was onto something here. We should tax ourselves, not for vice, but for our futures. Suppose you say, "I do not drink, gamble, or partake in vice." If you don't, that's great, but do you have a voluntary cable TV tax? Do you voluntarily drive a $459-a-month car where a $250-a-month car would do? If so, you are already "taxing yourself." You just need to redistribute the money to a more worthy cause: you and your family. The best way to "collect" the tax for you from yourself is like what the government does, first and often, and by electronic transfer from your paycheck or checking account to a prudent investment. The automation of the deposits is key. This is how the government acquires large piles of taxpayer money to redistribute. Take the concept and make it work for you.

> *Do you voluntarily drive a $459-a-month car where a $250-a-month car would do?*

Wilt Thou Tax the Very Air I Breathe?

The Colonialists fought against taxation without representation. Conservatives fought to repeal the death tax (taxation without respiration). Libertarians fought for no taxation without rationalization, which resulted in liberals and conservatives both showing us how to rationalize everything.

> *If you are thinking that government will take care of you, prepare for a rude awakening—government is planning on your taking care of it.*

In case you don't see a pattern here, let me be blunt: if you are waiting for someone else to take care of you, it's not going to happen. If your hope is in a mass movement, political party, or government, help is not on the way. If you are thinking that government will take care of you, prepare for a rude awakening—government is planning on your taking care of it. Without the withdrawals from our wages, the government could not exist. Only your blood (cash) transfusions keep the government pumping.

Yet somewhere between the tax-it-if-it-moves and regulate-it-if-it-stops crowd and the tax protestors comes a valuable lesson. It's simply this: we must tax ourselves over and above government's demands. Then we must invest the proceeds for our future and we must do this while soaring above the roar and din of the Libertarian versus conservative versus liberal battle for our attention daily. If the government pays itself first from our checks, shouldn't we at least do the same?

Problem?

So what's the problem? The problem comes in gaining traction and making our efforts fruitful in the day-to-day application of our plan. We may start a plan with great enthusiasm, and then get bogged down in the details and drudgery that must be worked through for success. It is the daily mixing of life's mortar and brick-by-brick effort that finally brings success. Have you ever watched a brick or block wall being laid up? It is not too exciting at first. Then as the corner leads are built up and the centers fill in, you begin to see the goal take shape.

To Be a Millionaire, You Must First Be a Thousandaire

Certainly having the first $100 in savings won't be too exciting. Even becoming a multithousandaire won't change your life, but by steady stick-to-it-iveness you will eventually become a one-, three-, four-, or five-hundred–thousandaire. Then you will notice that things can be a little easier. This is one reason that you need to take advantage of automated payments and savings deposits where possible. The computer pinging your paycheck to make a direct deposit in your Roth IRA or job replacement account does not grow weary. It doesn't get manic and depressive about the markets or lust over the new car ads. It just keeps marching forward. The automated deposits fill in for you when you might otherwise be weak.

Many of us take the train to Procrastination Station and set up housekeeping there. In the little town of Procrastination, everything is scheduled for tomorrow. Your only care is what not to do today. That $100 in savings is not so important; you can just save $200 the next time. Right? The difference between starting your retirement plan at age twenty and waiting until thirty is over $900,000. If you delay from age twenty to age

I never worry about retirement. I just put a dollar a
day in my Roth IRA and when I'm your age I'll have
$2,141,851. Maybe more if my mutual funds do well!

forty, the cost of procrastination is over $1,400,000 (source:
www.personal.fidelity.com). It's best we succeed in the small
things to get to the big things.

Longfellow wrote, "Most people would succeed in small
things if they were not troubled with great ambitions." This is
how most of us fail, by ignoring the small things—the simple daily duties of life that are really the building blocks of our greater ambitions.

> *Youth suffers from inexperience, while old age suffers from youth's inaction.*

Missed It by That Much . . .

Many of us die—or, worse yet, live—in the drudgery portion of life. Here's a secret: many of us are only a few feet from success. This financial death a "few feet from success" can come early in life if we quit pursuing our objectives. The awareness to develop a workable plan may come early or late in life. Priorities are the slipperiest members of the discipline family. The priorities of youth pose as good ideas for later. What should be priorities of our middle and later years are often confounded by the inaction of our youth. Youth suffers from inexperience, while old age suffers from youth's inaction. Begin! Think! The old man or woman can't ride the train if the youngster doesn't buy the ticket.

Why Aren't More People Successful?

If success is so easy, why don't more people succeed?" Jim Rohn replies, "Because it's easy to—and it's easy not to." The fundamentals of success are easy to apply—it is also easy *not* to apply them. It is human nature to stay the course, to bend toward the status quo—even if that course is not working. Billy Joel's hit song "The Piano Man" says, "They're sharing a drink they call loneliness—but it's better than drinking alone." In money matters, sometimes we stick to what is familiar to us even if it is fiscally imprudent. Plainly, many are comfortable in their bondage.

Samuel Smiles wrote, "Society at present suffers far more from waste of money than from want of money." It seems little has changed in over 130 years since his words were published. Foolishly, many of us do not build a base before we attempt to rise in the world. Many attempt to build a life on current income without providing a solid foundation or "putting some back" for the future. Still others, rather than building a base, borrow or mortgage their future with consumer debt or bad debt. Orison Marden said, "Don't risk your life's superstructure upon a day's foundation." Once the pattern of "make all you can, spend all you make" is set, many never find their way to freedom. Held hostage by their desire to look successful, they eat their seed corn. No seed, no planting—no harvest.

Suicide? Not Exactly

"Few men die," writes Dr. Marden in *The Conquest of Worry*. "Most kill themselves with worry." Together with procrastination, poor diet, and inadequate exercise habits, many of us add fear, doubt, and debt to worry. By the time we're forty, many of our definitions begin to change. Victor Hugo wrote, "Forty is the old age of youth; fifty is the youth of old age." Here is an exercise plan I have followed for years. First come the isometrics of resisting change. Second are the aerobics of jumping to conclusions. Third, I do strength training by stacking up heavy excuses.

Though it is fun to make light of diet and exercise, and a few comedians earn a living doing so, I want to assure you that neither diet and exercise nor money and debt are laughing matters if left unattended. When the laughter clears and we are left with the reality of the moment, we must realize that it's time to do something about our future.

> *Sadly, many of us offset every increase in income with new spending without regard to the possibility of outliving our money.*

The optimism of youth won't allow some to consider seriously that old age approaches with the certainty of gravity. Perhaps this fact won't resonate with you at age twenty or even age thirty, but by forty it should start to sink in. Given all of the advances in medical technology, odds are that you could live a long time. Each year the life expectancy tables stretch a bit and living hand-to-mouth seems less wise. On the average, we live thirty years longer than folks did one hundred years ago. The old witticism "If I had known I would live this long, I would have taken better care of myself" for our purposes could be "If I had known I would live this long, I would have saved or invested more money." Many allow Parkinson's second law—"Spending always rises to meet the income available"—to keep them broke throughout their lives.

Careful forethought is needed in developing a philosophy of how you earn, save, spend, give, take, lend, borrow, and bequeath. The goal of this chapter (and, indeed, this whole book) is to stretch your thinking. You could be with us for quite a while. Sure, things are going along swimmingly right now, but what if you live far longer than you anticipated? Sadly, many of us offset every increase in income with new spending without regard to the possibility of outliving our money. I am advocating not a starved or pinched existence, but a rational plan that allows you to be more than a greeter at Wal-Mart in your seventies or eighties. If you are a greeter at Wal-Mart by choice, that's fine. I'm talking about a senior citizen who has to make the choice between working and not eating. In every discussion of retirement or money, remember when to start saving: now! Sooner is better—but more sooner is best.

One More Book

I have forever been a one-more-book person, thinking if I read just one more book it could contain the Rosetta Stone that would unlock the universe of wealth and happiness for me. It turns out that the universe is already unlocked. The alleged secret is to begin. Just begin! In the last ten thousand pages I read while researching *Good Debt, Bad Debt*, I realized that there are no secrets to wealth and happiness. The answers lie in a few fundamentals: discipline, deferral, and discernment chief among them.

Many people long for a better life, yet head in the other direction mentally. To be successful, we must avoid the great disconnect between *knowing* and *doing.* Some of us read and study for years, thinking a little more knowledge is all we need to reach the Promised Land. Those who hold knowing or awareness to be equal to doing are forever lost. Some never turn graduation day into application day, when we apply what we have learned. The learning process is so satisfying for some that they fear stepping into the real world. "One talent fully developed is worth more than ten talents on a shelf," says Dr. Marden.

> *There are no secrets to wealth and happiness. The answers lie in a few fundamentals: discipline, deferral, and discernment chief among them.*

Better Late Than Never

I take great pleasure in reading and study. This is a habit I developed late in life. There is a word to describe it, *opsimath.* The prefix *opsi* is Greek for *late,* while *math* means *learning;* hence an opsimath is one who learns late in life. While we study, we must also be mindful that the "game clock" is continuing to run down. It's doubtful that your study will lead you to wake up near the end of your life with a plan to suddenly fill your retirement plan with all you need to replace whatever you do for income presently.

Work Is the Curse of the Consuming Classes

Oscar Wilde said, "Work is the curse of the drinking classes." Let's revise that statement to "Work is the curse of the consuming classes." If you agree, you probably are in the wrong career or leading a Consumerati lifestyle. Work feels like a curse if your "consumption set point" is positioned for someone with a larger income. The best situation is to find work you love and can make money at—and fix your consumption to fit your income. "I'm not fat. I'm just short for my weight," equates roughly to "I'm not broke. My income is just too short for my spending."

> *With Consumerati habits, if you hate your life while earning $30,000 a year, you will despise it at $110,000 a year.*

The planning and saving habits of the Econowise can scale to make you wealthy as your income increases over the years. The nonplanning and debt abuse habits of the Consumerati likewise can scale to make you poorer and deeper in debt as your income increases. Eventually the debt-obese develop Debtabetes. Even though they are making more and more, they spend more and more. Soon they lack the cash flow or financial insulin to break down and eliminate debt. In other words, with Consumerati habits, if you hate your life while earning $30,000 a year, you will despise it at $110,000 a year.

Part of this discernment involves finding work you love. Can everything you want in life financially fall into three neat headings? Maybe not, but most successful people I have interviewed about career satisfaction seem to have three things in common:

1. They live with people they love.
2. They are involved in work they love.
3. They operate a financial plan they love because it enhances the people and work they love.

The questions "how to," "why," and "for whom," are powerful motivators. Wait—so having a workable plan means doing what you love? Success is that easy? Let's assume that living with people you love makes your life more pleasant and aids in your overall success. I touch on some of this in Chapter 10 ("You Married Who?"). This section is about work and planning. The 2003 Spherion Emerging Workforce Survey of 3,200 full-time workers breaks down employees' intent as follows:

- 52 percent indicate a desire to change jobs, with 46 percent of them hoping to do so within the next six months and 75 percent within the next twelve months.
- 54 percent indicate growing confidence in their ability to earn a stable income outside the conventional work structure.
- 86 percent cite fulfillment and work/life balance as their top career priority; conversely, only 35 percent said that being successful at work and moving up the ladder are their top priorities.
- 73 percent of employees said that they are willing to curtail their careers to make time for family.
- 96 percent are attracted to employers who offer ways for them to make time for personal responsibilities and personal development, such as flextime, job sharing, and telecommuting.
- 81 percent work for employers who don't offer the work/life options they desire.

You can infer many things from these statistics. Of course, the first item (52 percent dislike their jobs) is interesting. Yes, what I am about to suggest is counterintuitive, but here it is: the more you dislike your job, the more motivation you should have to lower your burn rate and increase savings (so you can switch or quit jobs). If you don't strive to do this, you probably aren't serious about changing jobs. In the few years prior to 1981 when I left my "secure job," I had drastically lowered my burn rate and increased savings. Even though my first year in real estate amounted to a severe cut in pay, my expenses were so low that it really was not a problem. The Spherion poll says that 46 percent of those interviewed hope to make a change. Forty-six percent, that's an interesting figure—close to the percentage of people who are overburdened with consumer debt or pre-debtabetes. If they happened to be the same 46 percent, it would be hard to make a change, especially to a lower-paying job, even for a career you love, wouldn't it? It may be difficult to ever be truly successful in a high-paying job you hate.

Debt Makes Cowards of Us All

Think of the 46 percent who say they "hope" to make a change. It reminds me of the kids' riddle "Two frogs sat on a log, and one decided to jump. How many frogs are left?" (Answer: two. Just deciding to do something doesn't count. You need to actually jump.) When I was at Kroger and decided to leave, it took me four years to actually jump. My point here is that if you have a low burn rate, you can probably jump anytime and get all of the advantages the workers in the poll are saying they desire. Eighty-six percent say work/life balance is their top priority. It's hard to change careers if you are a slave to your past because of bad debt. Recall debt effect 1, loss of freedom. The past is the past, unless you still owe for it.

My prediction and experience is that employees who have a very low burn rate will be able to migrate to careers they love. Perhaps they'll take a lower-paying position for a time to be re-trained or finish an advanced degree and then achieve their bliss. The ultimate in all of this, of course, is to find work you love while keeping a low burn rate and applying the excess money toward a job replacement plan, also known as a retirement plan or (dare I say it?) an early retirement plan.

Years ago I heard Tom Hopkins say, "Most people are seven times more concerned with losing what they already have than with getting more." Here is an anonymous poem I have run across a few times, which illustrates well the sad effect of living half a life, of fearing to draw in a deep breath, as if afraid of choking on the air of opportunity. I first saw this poem in Dr. Dennis Waitely's book, *The Psychology of Winning:*

> There was a very cautious man
> Who never laughed or played
> He never risked—he never tried
> He never sang or prayed
> And when one day he passed away
> His Insurance was denied
> For since he never really lived
> They claim he never died.

We have a special life insurance policy on
Harold—it pays off "if he comes to life"!

Wealth Insurance

I suppose that one element of this poem would be an insurance underwriter's dream—an exemption that could avoid paying thousands of claims. While looking over this poem I had copied into my journal many years ago, I created the written concept of the cartoon you see here. Harold's policy pays if he comes to life.

Let's stretch this concept to the ridiculous so we can see the subtle lesson within. What if you had an insurance policy that paid off only when you really came to life and applied your full potential? You have your life insurance to pay your beneficiaries upon your death, but what if you live? With life insurance you have a great product, one you should not be without. But what's your backup plan? Suppose you live?

The insurance companies could safely use the known statistics: only 3 to 5 percent ever get close to what most people would define as success. Of course, the fine print would outline exactly what success is. Truly, who could argue that they have actually lived up to their full potential? I could not! Fully 95 to 97 percent of people do not succeed using the popular definition of *success*. Only 3 to 5 percent succeed in financial terms—while 100 percent die.

One thing is certain: Were such insurance available, to collect the benefits you would have to already be successful. If we assume that no such insurance will ever be available and that we are going to live a while longer, the question is, how then should we live?

> *"For my part, whatever anguish of spirit it may cost, I am willing to know the whole truth, to know the worst, and to provide for it."*

Patrick Henry said, "For my part, whatever anguish of spirit it may cost, I am willing to know the whole truth, to know the worst, and to provide for it." I see this as more a statement of maturity than a declaration of war. I remember early in life hearing, "True maturity is when you realize no one is coming to help." At some point in life, most of us leave whatever comfort we are accustomed to and fend for ourselves. That said, if help comes, accept it graciously, but don't become dependent.

Good News—"Wealth Insurance" Now Available

Actually, when you get the savings habit, you are really self-insuring your future. The premium on wealth insurance is equal to the amount that allows you to reach your financial goals in the time you have left before retirement. Many of us are willing to buy everything else on payments. Why not buy a future? Oliver Wendell Holmes said, "Don't put your trust in money—put your money in a trust." It doesn't necessarily have to be a complicated trust. It could be as simple as an IRA, Roth, or regular account with your local bank or brokerage. If you send e-mail to me at IRA@gooddebt.com, an autoresponder will send you a list of several self-directed IRA administrators. These are good if you wish to invest your IRA funds in something like real estate or perhaps mortgage notes (after you know what you are doing). If you are just getting started, using your local bank, a brokerage house, or mutual fund provider with a 1-800 number probably makes sense. As your needs grow, you can transfer your funds to another custodian or bank.

How Much?

Here are a few ideas of how much you need to save. If you wait until twenty years before retirement, the amount you are required to save will be much greater. I like to do the actual math, but one quick rule of thumb that many financial planners use is to take the desired amount per year you need to retire (in today's dollars) and multiply it by forty. If it's $30,000, you need to put back $1.2 million. If you want $50,000 per year in today's dollars in retirement, plan on putting back $2 million. This figure does factor in inflation and taxes. Many people I have talked to say that with a paid-for home and decent health, they figure about $800,000 in liquid assets will do.

The amounts needed could be different if a Roth IRA, a regular IRA, or another qualified pension fund was used. I have a close friend who says that the forty-times rule of thumb is way too high. He says $800,000 will take care of him. Ultimately, it depends on his after-retirement burn rate and the yield he earns on the $800,000. Your spending and lifestyle could change in retirement, and don't forget the extras like travel and grandchildren. Many retired couples find a serious increase in the food bill when they eat out more often. The sooner we begin our plan, the sooner we can reach the desired result. A couple I know are well on the way to a portfolio of twenty free and clear rental houses, a mortgage portfolio, and cash savings. Their estimated holdings come to $3.2 million. Everyone has different abilities. If you have $3.2 million earning a 3 percent yield, that is $96,000 per year. If the $800,000 is invested to earn 10 percent per annum, that's $80,000 a year.

This planning is different from death benefit insurance, where you must die before your family can collect. Here, so long as you live and make the deposits, the benefits increase and you eventually will be able to use them for retirement.

Years ago when I would speak of goal setting, I would often poll the audience by asking, "How many of you have life insurance?" About 70 to 90 percent of an audience would raise their hands. Then I would ask, "How many of you have specific written goals for what you want to accomplish in life?" Perhaps 3 to 5 percent would raise their hands. Then I would say, "The majority of you have a great plan—if you die. What if you live?"

Another Day, Another Dollar. That's Right, 4.2 Cents Per Hour.

Let's do the math beginning at birth for a twenty-year-old, a thirty-year-old, and a forty-year-old. I'll include starting at age fifty, the age when many wonder where the last thirty years went, to illustrate the example for procrastinators. For fun, let's say that we save $30 a month—the venerable dollar a day. Then below that we will assume that you need $800,000 in your wealth insurance plan (along with your paid-for house and a few other assets) to comfortably retire.

If you start on this type of policy at birth, let's assume that a parent gets the ball rolling while the cost is negligible. If you pay $1 a day ($30 a month) into your wealth insurance program from birth to age sixty-five, you will have over $2,000,000 if your sixty-five-year average rate of return was 10 percent. What if you have had neither the advantage of financially thoughtful parents nor the wisdom to start this plan on your own? The dollar-a-day plan (a euphemism for "save what you can") depends on starting at day 1 and never quitting. As much as the dollar, it is the habit we are developing.

Months to Age 65	Return Rate	Payment	Future Value
780 (age 0)	10%	$30	$2,327,277
540 (age 20)	10%	$30	$314,475
420 (age 30)	10%	$30	$113,899
300 (age 40)	10%	$30	$39,805
180 (age 50)	10%	$30	$12,434

What can we do if we missed this opportunity? Write an I-O-ME? I owe me $____ for my dollar-a-day fund? You could. Let's use the example of a child. Suppose you have saved little or nothing for your child, who is now eight years old. Simply calculate the number of days she has lived to get the principle and include 10 percent interest if you wish. In this case, an eight-year-old would be "owed" $2,920 (365×8=2,920 days) or $4,385 with interest. Plus you must continue to make the monthly deposits. Wait until you are forty years old and the makeup amount is $189,722 with interest.

Months to Age 65	Return Rate	Payment	Future Value
780 (age 0)	10%	$10	$800,000
540 (age 20)	10%	$76	$800,000
420 (age 30)	10%	$211	$800,000
300 (age 40)	10%	$603	$800,000
180 (age 50)	10%	$1,930	$800,000

Historians and Prophets

Here are just a few words about rate of return. In the first three years, don't worry much about return. Worry about developing consistency. Reread the first five chapters of *Good Debt, Bad Debt* if you need to. Especially think about burn rate and delayed gratification. The savings habit will save you. Inconsistency will kill you. I have seen interest rates for savings accounts range from a high of 16 percent to a low of 1.2 percent. You

> *The savings habit will save you. Inconsistency will kill you.*

do not know what the future will bring. A recent issue of *Money Magazine* touted mutual funds that had 30 percent growth in

2003. Don't labor over that kind of rear-view-mirror journalism. It's easy to write history. Prophecy is tough. You must buy a fund looking through the windshield. What you see in the rear-view mirror may not be the part of the river you buy. If you don't have the stomach for the stock market or mutual funds, consider real estate. Even with real estate, you need a great deal of education to make money.

One thing we must agree on: the savings habit is more important than the rate of return (yield). If you follow the recommendation of saving 10 percent of an average $52,000 salary for forty years ($5,200 per year), you will have over $2.3 million in your account. The average annual return of the stock market since 1926 has been about 10.7 percent. Don't let the Negative Neds of the world keep you from being in the game. There are some people who seem to have as their only purpose in life licking the chocolate off your Dilly Bar.

It Won't Work. Ned Said So.

The typical response of a Negative Ned to the chart above is "Ten percent! The rate of return is only 3 percent right now! You could never get 10 percent. The plan is no good." Negative Ned in 1981 (when rates were 16 percent return on savings) was saying, "No one can borrow any money! The rates are too high! Nothing will work at these rates." So no matter what Ned says, keep your Dilly Bar away from him and stay with your plan. It's the same plan at a 1 percent return on savings as at a 16 percent return on savings. We must accumulate capital at any rate to have enough to be able to participate in the better investments. If you can't save 10 percent of your income right now, save 5 percent. Ask Ned what happened to the people who had the savings habit ten or twenty years before 1981 hit. If you have a big pile of money when rates go up, you earn a ton of return on your capital. The men and women who stayed away from the Neds of the world and who accumulated, say, $50,000 by 1981 at normal rates had over $110,000 in 1986 even if they quit saving, which I would not recommend. I was not one of those, but I do know that you could invest in five-year CDs at over 15 percent yield in 1981–82. At 15 percent yield compounded annually, your money will double every 4.8 years.

Write It Down—Avoid Vain Proclamations

The first time you read anything on goal setting, you will probably notice the emphasis on writing things on paper. Writing down your goals is an essential part of the process, but becoming the type of person who can achieve your goals is the more important objective. Why do people hesitate to write down their goals on paper or in a journal? Because writing something down makes it real. Reality can be harsh. It disturbs the

> *Reality can be harsh. It disturbs the status quo.*

status quo. When we are making little progress or even regressing, we often allow ourselves a free pass by not documenting reality. The freeway of your mind has many exits and distractions. The reality of plans on paper makes it less likely that we will exit at Fantasy Land when we need to be in Reality City.

Basic goal setting comes in three parts: who will you become, what will you do to obtain your goals, and what do you want to own? You may remember these as BDO (be, do, and own). The verb forms are *being, doing,* and *owning.* Who will you become? What will you be doing to achieve these goals? What do you see yourself owning?

My goals radically changed as I grew older. Each day I now enjoy my quiet time to read, write, and reflect. This quiet time is usually not in a quiet place, though. I generally go to a Bob

Evans Restaurant or Panera Bread and tune everything out as I read or write. Fully 60 percent of this book was written at Panera. I probably developed the habit in 1994 as I studied for most of my college exams while downing massive doses of Bob's coffee. Though I have been in the real estate business for over twenty years, as I grew, started a family, and finished college at age thirty-seven, my desires radically changed. I finally admitted that my greatest nonhuman love was writing.

The one extra thing I want you to take from this chapter is how to be honest with yourself. Happiness will come and go, as it depends on circumstances (happenstance). True joy comes from purposeful work and operation of a plan with a knowable outcome. Jean Chatzky's book *You Don't Have to Be Rich* reveals surveys that show there is little correlation between happiness and income after the first $50,000. The road to joy may be as simple as dumping bad debt, lowering your burn rate, and being able to redirect (repurpose your life). This can involve starting a new enterprise or just being in a career you love.

Speak No Vain Truth

If you are trained in goal setting, you will hesitate to speak vain truths, because there are only two possible outcomes: (1) You fire a goal-seeking missile toward your dreams. (2) You become frustrated and the fungus of regret begins to grow. There really is no middle ground for a well-trained mind. Do not make hollow promises to yourself. Hollow promises only foment frustration. Brian Tracy says a lot of people live on "Someday Isle" ("Someday I'll be . . .").

I was not concerned about my writing ability; I was afraid that I wouldn't see the project through to completion. Would I be willing to do all of the work it would take to be a successful writer? Once I could honestly answer yes, then I was ready to begin. It has been well said, "If anything can stop you from writing, let it. If nothing can stop you from writing, then by all means write!" It took me a lot of years to get to the second part of that advice. Many are unwilling or unable to walk away from a twenty-year career. I found money and developed skill in the real estate business, but had no real joy. Perhaps I matured or just in the few hours a day I had for reflection I observed what others do and asked, What do I want to do with the rest of my life? We choose each day to be a slave of the past or master of our future (financially).

Perhaps many have the same fear about retirement funds as I've had about writing. Sure, it's easy to start, but will you see it through? Beginning is the most important part, most folks say. I say finishing the journey is the most important part. Beginning is fundamental, of course, but continuing is the only thing that brings the true result of wealth. If you are like me and have more beginnings than middles and ends, it's time to start concentrating on middles and ends. Automate your deposits or whatever you need to do, but have a beginning, middle, and end. Create a fully funded retirement plan.

> "The problem with being disgusted with where you are is that it keeps you where you are."

I'll Be Content When I . . .

So what makes a great life? I say contentment with and gratitude for what you presently have. There is great wisdom in contentment. This is not to say that you must stay where you are. It means to be content with what you have while you strive. Discontentment generally causes you to do things for the wrong reasons. Through the calm lenses of contentment and reason we are able to make wise choices. Back up a bit. Take a long-term look at your current short list of desires. Do they fit into your long-term plan? Do you even have a long-term plan?

Danger Will Robinson

If you are disgusted with life, recognize it as a danger signal. In January 2004, I wrote in my journal, half-joking (which is to say I meant it half-seriously), "The problem with being disgusted with where you are is that it keeps you where you are." We get more of what we pay attention to and subsidize. Truly, you get more of what you dwell on.

Education, Effort, and Enterprise—My Three Es

Burn rate determines fate; your spending will determine your ending. For most readers, spending habits will be their downfall. If you have an income problem, you address that through education, effort, or enterprise. A combination of all three brings the best results. Through education, you may learn a new trade or get better at what you are doing or completely change careers. Through effort, you may be promoted from where you are or you may work more hours if necessary. Through enterprise, perhaps you write, invent, or improve something to sell or start a new business. Sometimes your investments do well enough that you can pursue your enterprises full-time.

Ideally we follow a written plan for our lives based on discipline, deferral, and discernment. Once it's committed to paper and reviewed every few days, you will begin to notice results— if you also familiarize yourself with actual work and effort. Many people have a money-getting plan without a spending plan—they run roughshod over any true success they are so near by refusing to prioritize and control spending.

Wealth Metrics

How do I know if I have enough? Do I need to be wealthy? What exactly is wealthy? Henry David Thoreau and Buckminster Fuller both had some great things to say about wealth that you should commit to memory. Once you know how much capital will sustain your lifestyle, it is a matter of simple math and delayed gratification and prudent investments.

To paraphrase Henry David Thoreau, the cost of a thing is the amount of life I am willing to give up to pay for it. I have been at pains to show throughout *Good Debt, Bad Debt* that starting sooner is better and that small deposits early on will bring remarkable results. How much of your life are you willing to give up now to ensure a comfortable retirement? We are spoiled in America. Even a rather dull, poor life here is better than life almost anywhere in the world. Over and over studies show what people want more than more money is more time and balance of time for family life. Once you have money, time is what you want.

Buckminster Fuller, according to Brian Tracy, wrote, "Wealth is the number of days you can exist without working." This is the most useful definition of wealth I have heard. Ideally you want to be able to go without working indefinitely. Jack Miller of National Capital Corporation says that when he started his brokerage business, he would bank a year's worth of expenses as quickly as he could. In the early years it would take him nine months to get a year's worth of expenses saved, then six months. Then finally by the end of February or even January, he would have the year covered. Soon the cash flow from his investments covered all of his expenses. Jack says that when this happens, you are fireproof, as you never need a job again. Besides just freedom from toil, there are a few other benefits. One is freedom of time, which more and more Americans are beginning to place a high value on. Another is freedom of movement. The big freedom is in what you don't have to do. In a business transaction you don't have to bend to another's will, because your family is taken care of regardless of the outcome. People who have to make a "deal" usually don't make the best deal. When you don't have to make a deal to earn a living, this allows you to operate the simple system I spoke of in the beginning of this chapter.

Points to Ponder

- Retirement wealth is a product of time, accumulation, and discipline. Planning (goal setting) with a knowable beginning, middle, and end is the preeminent tool for success.
- Income is like a moving river; wealth is like a lake or reservoir. Stored income is wealth; spent income may not even bring fond memories. Review Chapter 3 ("Burn Rate").
- Work out emotions in the motivational portion of your planning.
- Don't allow an ever-increasing category of wants posing as needs to take away the possibility for gain. When you get that income increase, take care of your future first.
- Disposable income since the 1950s has increased nearly threefold (even when adjusted for inflation). We have expanded our desires so quickly that we miss the opportunity to take care of ourselves first and be free. Consider this analogy: Our poor eating habits shorten our increased life span. We shun a gift from modern medical technology because nearly two-thirds of us choose poor diet and exercise habits. Likewise, our giant increase in disposable income since the 1950s has largely been wasted. Instead of investing for our futures, we lust for every known consumer gadget and convenience known to man.

Chapter Seven

Real Estate:
Buy Five Houses—Get One Free!

Please release me, let me go . . .

The ten-second lesson: "Like the Lord, the real estate market helps those who help themselves. Unlike the Lord, the real estate market does not forgive those who know not what they do."
—James B. Wootton, past president of the Columbus Real Estate Exchangors, paraphrasing Warren Buffett

We often don't see opportunity because it is wrapped in difficulty or unattractive packaging.   —Jon Hanson

Of all the areas where you can profit from good debt, real estate may provide the most opportunity—if you are willing to become educated about valuation. Your eventual success or failure in real estate will hinge on your ability to find and recognize a bargain. You may accidentally make some money in real estate, but the odds are against it. Whether your real estate market is heading up or down, being able to discern value is the only way to profit from it. In the early 1980s there was a tremendous buyers' market. Cash was king. Tremendous bargains were available to those who had cash. Today common sense is king. Bargains are out there, but you are not facing an entire market ready to sell for cents on the dollar. It may take awhile to find the bargains.

Could you do this? Buy five of something for at least 20 percent under true market value and sell four of them at market or near market value? Then you move the profit forward each time until the money can pay for a house and you own it free and clear. Buy five, sell four. Easy, right? Perhaps you see problems with my example. There are a few: timing, taxes, costs of sale, market conditions, agents, brokers, lenders, discipline to reinvest, your perseverance, and your ability to discern true market value. If you can't discern true market value, how can you know if you are truly buying at 20 percent or more below value? Would you know a true Picasso painting if it was offered to you for some incredible price? I wouldn't. But if you give me a day, I can probably tell you if a single-family home in a given area is a good value—especially if it's in my town. With a little training, you may be able to do the same.

Either You Get It or You Don't

I hate to pull a Dr. Philism so early in the chapter, but it applies here. If you don't believe that you can do this, you are probably right. The sheer audacity to say that you may have a "free house" rubs a lot of people the wrong way. It sets up the classic pessimist-versus-optimist scenario. In my journal I have written, "Some ask if the glass is half-empty or half-full. I ask, 'Is it half-price?' " Let us remember that the objective here is to get a free house in a neighborhood you like. I am not talking about a $1 crack house from local government at the corner of Fear and Despair streets.

> *"Some ask if the glass is half-empty or half-full. I ask, 'Is it half-price?' "*

I may not recommend this technique for everyone. It takes a great deal of work to buy, sell, and trade houses—not to mention the extreme hassle of moving and the tenacity to carry out an eight-to-ten–year plan. I am often asked, "How can I get my house paid for quickly?" "Sell it," is the short answer, but "Buy it at a discount first," is the more complete answer. If you buy at a true discount, when you sell you will more than pay off the house—you will have a profit to apply to the next one. This process of buying and selling is a separate issue from just paying down your mortgage quickly. This free-house concept involves a bit of commerce. It is a large task. Ready?

Incremental Gifting

Instead of asking one person to just outright give you a free and clear house (but don't let me discourage you—you will never get without asking), we increase our odds of success and ease the pain for the donor(s) by just asking several to donate a slice off of four or five houses. Many people will throw in 5 to 10 percent or even 20 to 30 percent of the house free (the discount) if you will pay full price for the remainder. This is especially true if the seller is anxious to sell.

Let's use a nonhouse example. Suppose five friends and you are intent on buying Jiffy Deluxe Rice Cookers. Everywhere you shop they are $99 or more. You offer to pay the supplier $480 for a case of six Jiffy Deluxe Rice Cookers (that's $80 each after about 20 percent discount). He agrees. You collect $99 from each of your five friends and send the money to your supplier. When the cookers arrive, you deliver five to your friends and you have a free one for yourself. This is probably too much hassle for a rice cooker, but I think it illuminates the concept well.

Could you do the same thing with houses? Yes. Probably not in one swish of the pen, but over time if you bought five separate houses at 20 percent or more off, then sold them for full value, and kept plowing the money forward, the effect would be the same as we saw with the rice cooker (see the chart on page 145). Sometimes when the item is large or expensive, we are hesitant to haggle over price. When the price is large, there is more opportunity for gain. If you can haggle at a garage sale, you can make a low offer on a house.

Use a Coupon?

If you don't have your arms around this concept yet, think of it like buying a box of soap at Safeway or Kroger. You see a coupon in the paper for 25 percent off on Tide. What is the coupon saying? Isn't it really saying, "Bring in this coupon and pay the balance of 75 percent in cash and get this wonderful box of Tide"? Granted, most home sellers don't print coupons in the paper for 25 percent off (though this might be a good idea in a tough market). So you have to make up your own coupon. It's called a contract. Make an offer!

The deeper the discount on the coupon/offer, the fewer stores (sellers) there are willing to redeem it. How many offers (coupons) do you suppose you need to present to get a house at

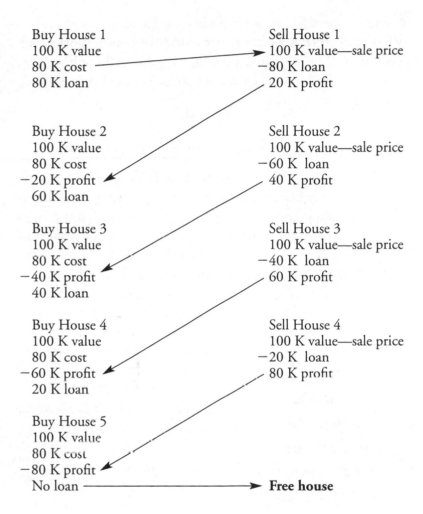

Buy House 1
100 K value
80 K cost
80 K loan

Sell House 1
100 K value—sale price
−80 K loan
20 K profit

Buy House 2
100 K value
80 K cost
−20 K profit
60 K loan

Sell House 2
100 K value—sale price
−60 K loan
40 K profit

Buy House 3
100 K value
80 K cost
−40 K profit
40 K loan

Sell House 3
100 K value—sale price
−40 K loan
60 K profit

Buy House 4
100 K value
80 K cost
−60 K profit
20 K loan

Sell House 4
100 K value—sale price
−20 K loan
80 K profit

Buy House 5
100 K value
80 K cost
−80 K profit
No loan

Free house

50 percent off? Let's add to the fun—assume you know little about real estate, but simply make offers at 50 percent of the market value. Even if you know a lot about real estate, this can take a couple of buckets of chutzpah. That's what I did in 1979 to buy my second house. It took sixty-nine consecutive refusals.

Some of the refusals came back with specific instructions of what to do with the offer that would have been physically impossible or at least quite painful. On the seventieth try, my coupon (offer) was accepted for 50 percent off. Painful, yes. Profitable, yes!

Don't Be Sad. Two Out of Three Ain't Bad.

Of the many real estate seminars I have been to, nothing I have learned has ever been worth more than this advice: write the offer. Stop talking and start writing. If you want to ask a girl (or guy) on a date, ask! If you want to buy a house, write! Mark Victor Hansen is fond of saying, "You don't G-E-T if you don't A-S-K!" One caution before you write the offer: be sure that you can discern value. When I was teaching real estate seminars in the '80s, I would often get a convoluted question about what I thought a seller would or wouldn't do. Don't analyze the seller; analyze his situation. My answer was always, "Write down your offer and hand it to the seller." If you have no training, get some professional advice from a competent broker or real estate attorney. He can help you with the proper contingencies such as a financing and home inspection. Be careful about overloading your contracts with contingencies, though. Your success rate will be much higher if you prearrange your funding for the purchase and make your offer plain and simple. If the house has a solid $100,000 value and you are offering $75,000 in an area you want to be

> *All sellers want the most money, the quickest sale, and the fewest problems. I say give them two out of three: quickest sale and fewest problems.*

in, why complicate things? Jerry Bresser says that all sellers want the most money, the quickest sale, and the fewest problems. I say give them two out of three: quickest sale and fewest problems.

A common problem people have is worrying about losing a deal on a home by making too low of an offer. My friend Jimmy Napier, author of *Invest in Debt*, says, "The ones that get away will never hurt you." If they don't like your offer, be polite. Say, "If your circumstances change, let me know." Then move on— daylight's burning.

Taxman

I assume that you will be living in these houses and planning to take advantage of the currently favorable tax law on resale. If you live in the property for at least two of the five years preceding a sale, the profits are tax-free up to $250,000 per person or $500,000 for married couples. Buying and selling houses, land, commercial property, or apartments as investments have very different tax consequences, which are beyond the scope of *Good Debt, Bad Debt*. If you are interested in this area, you will need to read about Internal Revenue Code section 1031 tax-free real estate exchanges. They are in truth tax-deferred exchanges. Later in life you may make use of charitable remainder unit trusts, for advanced estate planning and philanthropy.

The Good Debt Three-Step

The ultimate use of good debt is to capture and control profit. The concept of buying at a discount to capture profit, selling to realize the profit, and moving the profit forward is a tool that may be used in almost everything you purchase, especially investments. In my three Es (education, effort, and enterprise), this technique mainly involves enterprise but requires using all three precepts. You will always profit from applied education. If you are living in the house, the two years between sales will pass very quickly. What generally happens to me is that I am still remodeling when the two years pass, and I finish it up right before I sell. This three-step process will work on many different assets. In real estate, though, you have a product you may live in while doing all three steps (this increases safety). You may be able to squeeze through and make some money buying homes at 20 percent below the market if you live in them and keep your resale expenses low. The fact is, to do it very quickly, you will probably have to capture an even larger discount. With the costs of reselling, brokers, closing, and so on, reselling may take 10 percent or more of your sale price. Be sure to calculate a strong margin of safety into each transaction. Thus, if you are buying a $100,000 house for $75,000 and your actual costs of resale (selling for $100,000) do not exceed $5,000, you can still earn $20,000 to reinvest. Knowing the true value is critical. Learn values in the area you wish to invest in.

> *Use good debt to:*
> • *Buy at a discount to capture profit.*
> • *Sell to realize profit.*
> • *Move the profit forward (reinvest).*

The numbers in California will be different from those in Columbus, Ohio. The key is to learn the concept. "Buy five, sell four," can be applied to many things besides real estate. I used a form of this concept thirty years ago to buy, sell, and reinvest in cars. Of course, I started with a $22 car, a 1965 Chevrolet station wagon that was kind of a rust color if you know what I mean. In three years I had a current-model car that was paid for.

If you were in the car market from 1973 to 1976, you might remember how $150 would buy a decent, drivable used car. And for $600 you could get a really nice one. Many new full-sized cars were about $3,500 at the time. The numbers will be different today, but the percentages and the concept still operate no matter what the product.

> *I bought my first home when I was eighteen, so I was able to move that equity ahead a few times.*

In our first six years of marriage, Nita and I moved at least every year. I used to say, "We have been married six years, seven houses." I bought my first home when I was eighteen, so I was able to move that equity ahead a few times. I paid $23,600 for my first house in 1975 and walked away with about $6,000 profit four years later. Markets aren't always that favorable today unless you really grab a bargain. I have a close friend who paid $180,000 for his family's home in 1991 and eleven years later was looking at offers of $210,000 less costs of sale. I tried to buy the house next to him a few years ago and was blessed by not having my offer accepted. Sometimes the answers to prayers can be seen only in retrospect.

Chin Up

Do not be discouraged. Real estate always has bargains available, they may just be hard to see. Remember, it is a people business—not just real estate. It is this human element of real estate that gives opportunity for great profit. The fact is, you buy real estate from people, it gets used or rented by people, and when you sell it, you must entice another human or entity (controlled by people) to pay money to you. Don't worry so much about the market. Just become proficient in valuing houses in the area you want to live in, and work on your people skills.

If you have the valuation skills and people skills, all of the other skills, such as financing knowledge, can be added as you go along. How to properly value houses (or whatever you are buying) and how to get along with people are more important than an MBA from Wharton. I can think of a few MBA types I've dealt with who have turned wine into water in real estate deals.

The Three Circles of Debt

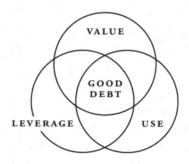

Circles of Debt

The circles-of-debt chart applies to all types of good debt, whether for education, real estate, or business investment. The value of any leveraged investment should safely exceed the market for the item.

> Test one: value. Does the value of your purchase exceed the loan by a safe margin? The use of good debt *must* be tied to lasting value, not consumption.
> Test two: leverage or loan. Will the loan self-amortize through the use, rental, operation, or resale of operating or reselling the asset? Are the terms beneficial to you?
> Test three: use. Is the item for income, resale, or utility? Do

you even need this item? Will it add to or subtract from your net worth? Is this something you can handle? Do you have the expertise, if it is a business? If it is education, can you apply your leveraged education in the marketplace for a profitable return? Based on use, income, or resale, is it profitable?

Say it with me: good debt is about value. In the case of hard assets, or real estate or business assets, rule number one is buy right and everything else will follow. In the case of borrowing for education make sure there is a market for what you are going into debt to learn. Yes, I am saying debt for real estate, businesses, or education is not always good debt.

The Key: Use Force If Necessary

The key to making money in real estate is to force inflation or an increase in value. This forced inflation can come by way of either sweat equity (you improve the property by making physical improvements) or finding a bargain. A third way is through regular inflation, though if everything else costs more when you arrive at the inflated price, did you really make any money? If your $50,000 house increases in value over the years to $100,000, but bread also goes from $1 to $2 a loaf, you probably are only keeping pace with inflation. On the whole, this beats renting under most any circumstances, especially if the rent on a similar house increases from $500 to $1,000 a month during the same period.

The problem with waiting for inflation to make money is that everything else you want to buy goes up while you are waiting. Don't misunderstand me, though. As in the bread example, we need things that will rise in value just to keep pace with inflation. That said, your net gain is best improved from forced inflation. For our purposes, if you benefit from long-term economy-based inflation, that's the gravy. Don't count on it. What I am advocating is to benefit from virtually immediate inflation by gaining as much discount as you can while purchasing. If you are a person who likes to fix up and remodel homes, it is a great justification for a big discount and a super way to make money.

Another possibility is to own property in the path of progress. In an area where major road construction and population shifts occur, you will benefit from the increase in values driven by the demand for the area. This is most prevalent in commercial property, but residential housing may benefit also. This too is forced inflation, though it is inflation not driven by you. Be careful acting on local rumors or neighbors' advice. I sank a big chunk of money into an up-and-coming area (one with a new freeway exchange) and would rather have my money in something more productive right now. Once you figure the holding costs, interest, and lost opportunity cost, you may change the way you feel about the deal. It is painful to have three-year money in a ten-year project. I'm a little off the track here as this is a commercial project with rezoning and a lot of twists and turns. Nevertheless the same will go for a home to live in. Be careful to verify information with state and local officials and not rely too heavily on rumor. You will always do better to make your money buying at a discount. Excellent negotiating skills plus the ability to rally the troops to do improvements could be the best combination. I cannot overemphasize the need for people skills in real estate. If you are married, you know that from time to time people do irrational things.

It's Not Broken—It's Not Perfect Either

Real estate's value can be certain only when a willing and able buyer is ready to pay the cash (or whatever a seller will accept) into escrow for a deed.

For all of the cars and houses I have traded, the one thing I love about it is the imperfect market, meaning the buyer and seller can agree on pretty much whatever they want. If every house on Elm Street is selling from $140,000 to $161,000, nothing except a prior commitment of a lien or mortgage can keep Joe Seller from selling 12 Elm Street to Ima Buyer for $98,000.

If you cannot imagine buying a house or anything else for 20 to 50 percent or more off, you will never be able to do it. You must stretch your mind to get there. If you are not the fixer-upper type, you will have to "look for the couple with a crack running through the marriage instead of the dining room ceiling," says Barney Zick, author of *The Negotiating Paradox*.

Sometimes people sell to others at a bargain price because they like and trust them. In 1982, I took over the payments on a house in Gahanna, Ohio, by paying about $3,200 for the seller's equity. This amounted to $1,200 cash in back payments and giving the seller a note for $2,000. At the same time I was negotiating to buy this property, another investor I knew offered the seller $5,000 cash for his equity. The seller told me that he did not like and trust the other guy. The $5,000 story was later confirmed directly by the late Nick Koon, my friend and competitor. The point I am making here is that the seller took my offer because he liked and trusted me. I foolishly sold the house too soon (1985) when I was in a self-inflicted cash flow crunch. This house was a rental, but the concept would have been the same for an owner-occupied unit.

"Boy, if I saw a deal like that, I'd jump on it!" says the average citizen. Would you? When Joe Seller decides for whatever reason to knock 35 percent off his price, he wants to have his money quickly. Many are unable to take advantage of the opportunity because of bad debt. Here is debt effect 4, lost opportunities, from Chapter 1 ("The Debt Effects"). As I said then, when you see a great opportunity, it is unlikely that you will be able to take advantage of it, because you will be financially unable to do so. Funds already spoken for must remain silent when opportunity knocks.

> *It is a vicious thing some writers do, to excite the minds of readers with the big profits available in real estate while downplaying the work and the risks required to make such returns.*

Think!

It is a vicious thing some writers do, to excite the minds of readers with the big profits available in real estate while downplaying the work and the risks required to make such returns. Consider this paraphrase (we changed *stock* market to *real estate* market) of a famous Warren Buffett quote about the stock market: "Like the Lord, the real estate market helps those who help themselves. Unlike the Lord, the real estate market does not forgive those who know not what they do."

While buying and selling four or five houses for profit will not require the genius of Einstein, it will require no less diligence. Additionally, just because someone says a house is worth $140,000 may not make it so. At a minimum you will want to look at what other properties have sold for in the area. If they are all square-box tract homes with a variety of just two or three kinds, the comparison may be easy. Even then an appraiser must take into consideration the extras. Many of the things people do to "improve" their homes may not bring the return they had planned. Generally, fresh paint, landscaping, and new kitchens and baths have the highest return. In the Midwest and all parts north, good windows or replacement windows usually add value to the resale. Real estate trainer Jerry Bresser says, "Paint is worth $10 in the can and $1,000 on the house." Of course, the days of $10 paint are gone.

One thing is for sure: nothing can increase the value of a house like cleanliness and elimination of unnecessary junk. In 1988, we bought a house for $37,000 that soon sold for $61,500. What did we do? First, we cleaned and painted the entire house inside and out. My painters were my wife, nieces, cousins, nephews, relatives, and anyone foolish enough to stop by and ask what we were doing. We spent about $1,000 hauling away junk cars, engine blocks, trees, shrubs, and everything else you can imagine. We added new carpets and spent $2,500 on seven replacement windows. I suppose that I spent $5,000 to $7,000 in all. This house really was the proverbial worst house on the block in a decent neighborhood. Other neighbors were thanking us for cleaning and fixing it up. After twenty-two years of no paint or cleaning, it was pretty grungy. The point is that everything we did to it was cosmetic. The problems looked enormous, but all were easily correctable.

Here is a timeworn and true list of things that bring back your money when you are ready to sell:

- *Curb appeal.* Clean and repair driveways, walks, patios, and landscaping.
- *Kitchens and baths commensurate with the area.* Corian counter-

tops will not return the large investment in moderate-priced housing.

- *Maintenance-free exteriors.* Energy-efficient windows, vinyl siding, and aluminum siding are generally preferable to clapboard or painted shingles, unless you are in an area trying to do original restorations. Then vinyl and aluminum are a detriment. In most areas a brick house will sell more quickly than any other type.
- *New paint and carpets.* These two inexpensive interior items always help sell a house.
- *Supercleanliness, inside and out.* Even if your prospective buyers are slugs, they will want to start out in a clean house.
- *Clutter-free counters, closets, basements, and garages.* Here's one time when it is good to rent a storage unit if needed. A large room with too much furniture looks small. A wide-open basement looks gigantic. Have you ever tried to look at a basement and only seen the tops of boxes?
- *No pet odors.* You may acculturate to the smell of your pet and not be aware of it. If you are not sure, bring in someone objective to tell you if there is an odor that needs to be dealt with. Cats and dogs are great, but I have seen prospective buyers literally get sick from a pet's odor and never consider that house again.

Who Can Find Bargain Real Estate?

If you are the type who never goes to Home Depot, you may have to take a very different approach from the handyman types. I truly believe that most people will have a skill or can develop one that will help them through their four or five bargain homes.

Let's look at a few possible types.

Contractors. This should be a no-brainer, but you would be surprised how many in the construction trades do not buy and sell the products they work on daily. It would occur to me that a house framer could frame a house for a concrete-and-foundation man, and the concrete guy could build a foundation for the framer. Most of these guys know all the right folks to do the entire job, but never seem to do it. A very large portion of a house is labor. Also, don't forget to think across various categories. I once traded my skill at setting up Web sites for concrete work.

Accountants and Lawyers. These people have skills that may help you negotiate, though the accountant may analyze the deal until it is gone. An accountant or lawyer may hear of a potential bargain long before the general public does. So long as a professional does not use privileged information gained from a client to the client's detriment and the professional's gain, she is like anyone else out there looking for a bargain. With enough disclosure, you can probably do about anything. The safest thing, though, would be to buy your bargains from a referring professional.

Car Salespeople and Horse Traders. Chutzpah is abundant. Making offers is the best way to buy houses. In general, car people (the ones who last) have thick skin and are used to being looked down on and scorned by the public. Rejection rolls off their backs, and the good ones persevere, understanding that one hundred offers will eventually get a house at 20 to 50 percent off. A

> *Use what you have to get what you want.*

good car salesperson will also understand trading and underallowing (giving credit to seller at less than full value) on a trade-in house. A proficient car salesperson will understand all of the above and use push cars (cars bought in the market below wholesale) as part or his or her entire offer to buy real estate. I have used cars to buy real estate and have accepted cars as a down payment on real estate. This again is a lesson for all of us. Use what you have to get what you want. If you can, trade cars (or anything) you buy in the marketplace for 60 to 70 percent of what a seller will credit you on real estate. Isn't that the same as buying the seller's real estate for sixty or seventy cents on the dollar? Would you necessarily have to actually buy the cars before you offered them? Say no. Could you pay for the cars with a 60 or 70 percent loan on the real estate you are buying? Say yes.

Bookworms and Computer Geeks. It is an information age, so you can probably use the Internet to search counties for real estate information in all fifty states. For some counties you can find data on comparable sales, square footage, and types of financing as well as current pictures and even copies of mortgages. When you are an expert at doing title searches (you will need to do some at the courthouse), you are in a position to have all the information needed to make a quick decision on a property. I remember in the '80s being able to get a quick title search over the phone from a friend at a title company, which allowed me to make an immediate decision on a property. This information enabled me to beat out competing buyers the seller had called from various "cash-for-your-home ads." I was able to make a deal on the spot and close in seventy-two hours. While there is a lot of information online, it is not infallible. It is also not guaranteed. The seventy-two–hour period in the above example was to give me time to get title insurance issued.

Firemen. Firemen are some of the hardest-working people I have ever met. Many have unusual schedules, such as twenty-four hours on and then forty-eight hours off. I know many who have little side businesses of buying, fixing up, and selling houses. They seem to be ultimate handyman types. Most firemen I have met are personable and friendly, which aids them immensely in dealing with buyers and sellers.

Grocery Clerks, Waitresses, and Everyone Else. No matter what your line of work, you will be around people who are buying, selling, looking for, or inheriting real estate. Bresser says, "Everyone is someone or knows someone that is buying or selling real estate or thinking about buying or selling real estate." Don't allow yourself to get into the mindset that a person serving you at a restaurant or the busboy doesn't own real estate.

Where Should I Start?

Read My Lips: Start in a Starter Home. Is there a more pliable term than the phrase *starter home?* The very words give different people different pictures in their minds. In undefined speaking or writing, it's as useful as the phrase *living wage,* which many of our politicians love because it means very different things in Los Angeles and in Hardscrabble, Ohio.

What is more appealing: 3,000 square feet mortgaged or 1,600 square feet free and clear?

I'm going to guess that a lot of my readers already own a home. I meet many people who think that I am quite insane to recommend moving every two years. It is tiring but profitable. I am down to about a seven-to-ten-year cycle now.

To some, burrowing in and paying for fifteen or thirty years seem quite natural. This is a good option too, especially if you find an area where homes appreciate more than in surrounding areas. In the Columbus, Ohio, market, those that burrowed in a home in Bexley or Arlington probably have done quite well.

With the current tax law on personal residences, you can sell every two years and owe no tax on the gain. You can then move up or down, rent, or move to New Zealand. The old personal residence tax rules required you to trade up in value each time to stay tax-free (but you did not need to stay any minimum time). Naturally many people want to move up—but eventually you may want to downsize. The average life span is close to eighty. How many eighty-year-old couples need a 2,800-square-foot two-story? If the house brought $300,000 tax-free and you bought a one-floor, well-situated home for $160,000, could you

The Pulleys bought it in 1963 for $15,900. The Gerkes bought it in 1970 for $32,900; the Smiths, in 1975 for $61,000 (they got divorced). It went to foreclosure in 1983, bringing $75,000. Two guys fixed it up, added a garage, then sold it in 1989 for $125,000, so you can see what a bargain it is at only $214,900 today!

find something to do with the extra $140,000 tax-free? Say, you go from 2,800 square feet to 1,600 square feet. This could be a wise move. Even if you owed money on the bigger property, perhaps the profit from the sale could make the new home free and clear. You do not always have to trade up. What is more appealing: 3,000 square feet mortgaged or 1,600 square feet free and clear? You might also read my definition of neutral debt in Chapter 1 ("The Debt Effects") as it pertains to home mortgages. The fact that a debt is a home mortgage does not automatically make it a good debt.

Right-Size That House. In the past I was an advocate of always trading up and perhaps owning a starter mansion eventually. Over the years as I learned more about money and real estate, I found that strategy to be very expensive. Most small families don't require 3,000 to 7,000 square feet of finished living area. My heart just wasn't in owning a $500,000 house. In 2003, the average home in our area cost $177,500. When we last moved a few years ago, Nita and I had plans from 1990 (from before the era of our IRS problems; see preface) for a two-story home of about 3,100 square feet. We took those plans and had a designer convert it to a ranch home. We didn't use the plans in the end, but from there we came up with what was important to us. Here are a few of the things we discerned from spending a lot of time and money trying to design the perfect home (none are perfect):

1. We needed about 2,000 square feet or less of actual living space.
2. We needed massive amounts of storage space that could be cheaper to build than the finished living space. Calculate how much you spend for a mini storage unit per foot.

3. We were sick of small garages. Are your cars outside while the garage is full of junk or projects?
4. Porches should cover all of the entryways and be deep enough (eight feet) to use.
5. The entire exterior would be maintenance-free materials.
6. We would spend extra for premium windows and doors.

The Basic House

Nita and I decided that the solution to the actual living space would be a ranch home with about 2,200 square feet. Most of the storage would be in a full dry usable basement with four walkout windows. We used Superior Walls of Ohio for the basement to get a ten-foot interior height and insulation. This gave us 2,200 square feet in the basement that was warm and dry. Superior also made a stairway from the basement to the garage as well as the low walls for the garage foundation.

Garage-Zilla

Framing a 28×50×12-foot-high garage with two 16×8 garage doors and three walk doors solved the garage problem. To recap, we ended up with 2,200 square feet of finished living area plus 2,200 square feet of warm, dry basement with lots of natural light and plumbing roughed in for future baths if we wish. We also built 736 square feet of porches and a 1,400-square-foot garage. In this example I was the builder and contractor. Garages cost $14 to $20 a square foot. Houses cost $50 to $75 a square foot. Basements cost $8 to $12 a square foot. I don't know if you can build a house for these figures in your area. While all of the concrete, brick, and skilled labor were from outside sources, I was involved in the labor in many areas of this house—more than I ever care to be again. An engraved stone in the brick near a garage entrance says *Ancora Imparo*, which is Latin for "Still I am learning."

You Gotta Live Somewhere

If you are living free somewhere, perhaps still with your parents and not saving as much as it would cost to rent a decent place, you are being very foolish. I know of twenty-somethings who spend upwards of $30,000 a year on trinkets and baubles and never save anything— even while living off Mom and Dad. If you are eating out of Mommy's refrigerator and not paying rent or banking a majority of your earnings, you are training a vicious appetite that will someday bite you. If you cannot save 50 percent of your income while someone else feeds and shelters you, you are well on your way to a lifetime membership in the Consumerati. This is because of the habits you are training. Think of this 50 percent savings rate as building up your financial muscle to leave the nest. If

> *If you cannot save 50 percent of your income while someone else feeds and shelters you, you are well on your way to a lifetime membership in the Consumerati.*

you can set aside your youthful omniscience for a moment, you will see how wise this can be. Not only will you acculturate to spending habits you can live with; you will have capital to start your new life away from the shackles of debt.

Let's discuss the folks who do not own a house. The vision they usually have is somewhere above the much maligned starter home.

I assume that you are having no problem paying the rent where you are. If this is true, then take what you are paying in rent and see how much you could apply to a mortgage. Let's use an example of $650 a month in rent. If you could qualify for a loan at 7 percent for thirty years, that would give you a buying power of $97,000 approximately. Of course, you will have to pay real estate taxes and insurance in addition to the $650 principle and interest. If you buy your house at a great enough discount, you may not need a down payment.

Up Debt Creek Without a Paddle

Most people get into bad debt by thinking emotionally instead of critically. You can see and hear examples almost everywhere in our society.

The trip up Debt Creek is an emotional trip. Recently I listened, actually eavesdropped, as a couple buying a home were trying to decide between upgrade cabinets and hardwood flooring. They could qualify for a loan only to get one or the other.

For this couple, making this choice wasn't a rational decision. It was an emotional choice because they were at the end of their income. The decision might have felt rational to this young couple, but it was emotional. If they were thinking rationally, they wouldn't have even considered the upgrades. If you have no margin for error, you probably are making a bad debt decision.

> *Why consider Baltic Avenue when we can finance our way onto Park Place?*

In *The Millionaire Mind*, Tom Stanley discusses an "easily affordable home." He says that if you have ever owned an easily affordable home and continue to do so, that is an indicator of your eventual success. What's an easily affordable home? Stanley says it is one that you could easily make the payments on even if your income was cut in half.

I can imagine a few egos mumbling, "I certainly wouldn't want to live in a place like that! I deserve better!" I agree, if you earn it, and the way you get better is to begin in a starter home. Few people are willing to start with a starter home. Why consider Baltic Avenue when we can finance our way onto Park Place? Emotions take over, common sense is chucked overboard, and you qualify down to your last eight dollars a month.

The rationalization usually sounds like this: "We are going to be in this house forever, so we should get what we want, even if we have to pay a little more." Statistically you're not likely to be in the home for even seven years. Success is at hand if you strive to put in the effort to profitably climb up from a rational beginning. Popular culture teaches us to value comfort over sensibility. Gratification needs to be fulfilled, well, immediately, doesn't it?

The Key to Success: Buy Right—Get a Good Deal on the House

Generally, as a guideline for lenders, 29 percent of your gross income is allowed for housing expenses. This can be moved as high as 41 percent if you do not have other debts. If you are earning $50,000 per year, you could have a housing expense of up to $1,200 a month. Depending on your taxes and insurance payments, this could put you in a $150,000 house when interest rates are 7 percent.

Many books are written on financing. It's an important subject you need to know. While you are excited about getting a 5 percent loan on a home and seeing how much more house you can afford because of a favorable interest rate, don't lose sight of the price of the home. Instead of getting abused by price or financing, strive to make both work for you.

You may improve the financing later. But you won't be able

to go back to the seller for an improvement of the price and say, "Obviously I paid too much for the house. Can you give me back some of my money?"* The first mortal sin in real estate is paying too much. The second is not recognizing a good deal when it is right in front of you. The third sin is not getting along famously with people. You need people to buy real estate.

Is it worth all of the effort to think, plan, and search for five bargain houses? That is really a question you can answer only in retrospect. When you see a friend labor under the pressure of paying a 95 percent loan to value payment, while over the past ten years your payment has gone from reasonable to zero, then you can answer.

I bought it as a fixer-upper,
but it became a never-doner.

*An exception is when the seller is financing you. Then you may ask every few months or years for a discount of the note the seller holds (which would be effectively a reduction in the overall price and basis of the home).

Points to Ponder

- Improve your people skills and make offers. You don't buy real estate from a market. You buy real estate from people. The condition of the market is secondary.

- Right-size your home and provide for storage on-site. Small storage units often rent for as much as $14 per square foot per year. A 10×10 mini storage unit for $85 a month or $1,020 a year goes for $10.20 per square foot. That $10.20 per square foot is a good start on building a garage.

- Buy right. Don't fall into the trap of a builder that buys down a rate for you and marks up the house to cover it. A buy-down is when a builder or seller allows his bank to collect interest in advance that is added to the cost of the loan (and the price of what you are buying) to give you a low payment for the first few years. A buy-down is a gift you pay for. Be a value-based investor. Be the Ben Graham (author of *The Intelligent Investor*) of real estate on your block. In the late '70s and mostly through the '80s, Robert Allen (author of *Nothing Down*) said, "Don't wait to buy real estate. Buy real estate and wait." And it was good advice for the times. But no matter the market, buy right or don't buy. Today I would say, "Don't wait to buy real estate if the price is great."

- Read and learn all about financing. But in your hurry to put into practice what you have learned, don't fall into the trap of being highly leveraged. Ask, "Do I want to be wealthy or look wealthy?" In the fullness of time you can be both. Remember my Buffett paraphrase: "Like the Lord, the real estate market helps those who help themselves. Unlike the Lord, the real estate market does not forgive *those who know not what they do.*"

Warning: If you want to get into real estate investing as a business, it requires even more knowledge than buying and selling a few houses to live in. If you are intent on doing more than buying low and selling high and living in the properties during the process, get a lot of training and practical knowledge first. See www.gooddebt.com for a few recommendations. Look at the notes on the Web site for this chapter. And beware. There is a class of real estate investors and wholesalers out there that prey on the inexperienced and their enthusiasm. This is a battleground not to go into unarmed. Recall the old bromide, "If it sounds too good to be true, it probably is." Be suspicious of someone who wants to hand you a prepackaged deal that you will supposedly make big money on. Another treacherous path involves a promoter who wants to use your good credit to "refinance" a property and then you will own the property or he will sell it for you. Houses, like convenience foods, always cost more when they are prepackaged and processed. I have seen a few people go through some pretty painful "processing."

As a rule, if you put together a nothing-down or creative transaction and know what you are doing, it is probably all right. If someone wants to hand you a fabulous deal, you have to ask yourself, Why? Deal directly with sellers that need to sell, and use an attorney and/or an appropriate real estate professional.

Chapter Eight
Driving Your Life Away:
Are You Driving Your Retirement into the Ground?

It's the only thing they had that would haul the payment book!

The ten-second lesson: "The average new car loses value at a rate of approximately $250 per month or more in the first few years of service. Coincidentally, this is the exact amount most of us should be putting into a Roth IRA."   —Jon Hanson

A November 25, 2003 Wall Street Journal *article revealed that the median car payment in the United States is $383. Edmunds.com says that it is $447. Many are $600 or more per month. Given that less than one-third of Americans are saving enough for retirement, shouldn't this give us some ideas?*

Car salesmen have twisted more emotions and broken more hearts than Sandra Bullock and Tom Cruise combined. Yet we continue to flock to the showrooms like flies to a bug light. By definition, debt for a car is bad debt. It is a loan on something that decreases in value. It only takes your money. Think not of $599 a month, but of $7,200 a year. How big of a percentage of your income is that? If you make $45,000 a year, it is a big portion. Even if you pay cash for your car, truck, or SUV, it still depreciates at a rate of $250 or more per month.

Cars are commodities. For nearly two-thirds of Americans, cars represent a payment that is included in their burn rate. Until you can pay cash for your vehicles, the best advice is to keep the expense moderate. When I hear of average folks spending 20 percent of their gross income on car payments, I know that there is little hope for their early retirement. If the car eats 20 percent, the housing expense is 38 percent, and the government takes up to 38 percent, not much is left, is there?

Have you ever been swayed by the advertising from car manufacturers? Sadly, I have. They are pretty good at it, aren't they? Men may be influenced by the odd combination of fenders and flesh, while women are gently reminded of an image they should conform to. Once the manufacturers have run the gamut of stars, cars, and flesh, they begin to tug at your heartstrings with safety, environmental responsibility, fulfillment (you pick the type), or Madison Avenue's favorite, keeping up with your "reference group." They don't even need to use words. When you see the handsome young executive pull into the garage and his supermodel wife and his picture-perfect children greet him ever so lovingly at the door (words are not required), you know that you need a Lexus. The same ad for women would have the professional woman coming home to the house-hubby asleep on the couch with toys strewn all over and a voice-over of "In your fast-paced life at least you can count on your Lexus not to let you down." As for car ads, I personally respond better to a safety message than one designed to appeal to my virility or vanity. I appreciate the safety message in automotive ads; it's important to me. The last time a drunk driver went left of center and hit me, I was glad to be in a Lincoln Town Car and not a gas-saving Yugo. Most cars from model year 1992 and later will have the basic safety options, such as air bags and ABS brakes. There are some dollars (such as last-dollar fuel economy) on the table I don't want to save.

Everyone Needs a Car!

I cannot think of a scenario where debt for a car would be considered good debt (except, perhaps, certain business applications). Cars are at best a commodity, a part of your burn rate. While they are part of your burn rate, excessive debt for cars is bad debt, by definition. This is debt that is robbing you of your future. Few of us want to admit that our probable lack of retirement savings has to do with our spending habits. One fellow told me that if he didn't spend it on his car, he would spend it somewhere else! Good point. I asked him if he is willing to buy everything else on payments, why not buy a future? He was still mesmerized by the smell of the virgin leather in his new Japanese sedan. I took a whiff and must admit that my faith began to weaken. It was very alluring. I pulled my head out of the car and asked, "This car is how much a month?"

> *If your desire to be successful financially cannot trump your vanity, this will be a difficult chapter for you. Yes, Virginia, you need a car. But not a $599-a-month car.*

He said, "It's $599."

"And a Taurus or Camry would be how much?"

"Under $300, I suppose."

"And how old are you?" I queried.

"Thirty-one."

"That's $300 a month that could be redirected and more profitably 'employed' in a retirement or investment account, right?" I pointed out.

"Yes," he replied. "But you mean I live without the virgin leather?"

I responded, "Yes, but look at what you do get: $300 a month for thirty-four years (you are then sixty-five) in a reasonable investment turns into $1,027,616.83."

"You mean my $50,000 Lexus is costing me over $1 million?"

Actually, the total cost is over $2 million in thirty-four years if you consider the whole $600 a month. That's sickening! The $1 million is merely the difference between the $300 and the $600 per month over thirty-four years.

Yes, Virginia, there is a Santa Claus. No, Virginia, he is not bringing you a free car. Yes, Virginia, you need a car, but not a $599-a-month car. If you are earning an average income, you could profit by having a less-than-average car payment; none at all would be even better. That said, I am making the generous assumption that you actually do the right thing with the money saved in lower transportation costs. The average payment of $383 per month for a car is more than 10 percent of the average worker's yearly after-tax salary. Can you drive less of a car and have low or no payments? The short answer is yes. The more difficult answer is maybe—if you are willing to learn not to care about having the latest-model car with all the newest options. Can you wear no-name jeans? I know some people who can't. If your desire to be successful financially cannot trump your vanity, this will be a difficult chapter for you.

The Gardner brothers of Motley Fool fame advise the obvious: "Buy less and drive it longer." The Fools are right, at least if you desire to deploy your money in more productive pursuits. Few things in life fade as quickly as the "new-car high." To some, it can be addictive, requiring even more investment to get "high" the next time.

> **"Buy less and drive it longer."**

From long experience I know that you can greatly increase the life of your chariot with regular oil changes (every 2,000 to 3,000 miles), changing the transmission fluid and filter every 25,000 miles, and rotating tires every 6,000 miles. Practicing what I call guerilla maintenance—that is, fixing everything as it comes and when it comes up—will enhance the likability of a car too. Don't give yourself opportunities to justify wanting a new one when you really don't need it.

If you enjoy doing your own maintenance, so be it. If not, quick-oil-change places are plentiful; they are located near most white-collar population bases. I don't find it worth the time or the tiny net savings to do much of this maintenance myself.

My friend Marv says that he never has had car payments. He started with an old car to drive and then saved what would have been a car payment. As the money accumulated, he bought a slightly better car and eventually a new one for cash. Marv's plan is really smart. It employs all three Econowise virtues: discipline, deferral (delayed gratification), and discernment. If you drive an old car and bank the average payment, once you build up to $30,000 or so, let me know if you go out and spend it all on a car. This should be the true indication of how badly you really wanted that new car. Once you have the money in hand

and have studied how quickly cars depreciate, you might want to consider letting someone else absorb the high cost of the "new-car smell" for the first two or three years. According to *Automotive Lease Guide*, even a stellar performer like a Honda Accord LX with a manufacturer's suggested retail price of $20,950 (approximately) depreciates at roughly $250 a month over three years. Isn't that a very high cost for fifty-seven minutes of happiness? This is a $250-a-month decrease in value plus the cost of the car and any finance charges. Looking at a copy of *Black Book Official Used Car Market Guide*'s weekly edition as a guide to what dealers would pay for a used Accord, we recall that *Automotive Lease Guide* had it at 45 percent depreciation over three years. We find that in the first year the car depreciates 20 percent. The rate slows to 11 or 12 percent in years two and three. The wholesale price after a year for a Ford Taurus is $10,300 versus $16,300 for the Accord, but to be fair you can buy the Ford for approximately $16,000 new. The Honda will cost you about $20,000 after discounts. They both have an MSRP of about $21,000. I am not an advocate of either Ford or Honda—I am an advocate of putting the $250 a month you would spend on depreciation toward your retirement or job replacement plan.

While debt can take the waiting out of wanting, sometimes debt takes the purpose and common sense out too. I suspect that many people who would spend a few years accumulating the savings might just buy another used car—a paid-for two- or three-year-old car or truck allows you concentrate on more important things. I have the feeling that you will like the money in the bank better than the smell of a new car. If you become inspired to pursue the Econowise lifestyle, the satisfaction of operating your plan will exceed any temporary thrill you can derive from a new car or truck.

No, no, no! I said you've got to have a PURPOSE!

A Real Looker

If a car is a fashion statement for you, just admit it and budget for it. For many people, that's what cars are. You may have to find the money you need in another area. Neil Fiske and Michael Silverstein, in *Trading Up: The New American Luxury*, write, "Almost everyone (96.2 percent) will 'pay more' for at least one type of product that is of importance to them, and almost 70 percent identified as many as ten categories in which they will rocket—that is, spend a disproportionate amount of their income, as compared to spending in other categories."

Cars, trucks, and SUVs are commodities that are continually depreciating. If this is an area you feel you need to "rocket" in, just be realistic about counting the cost. A new car may bring short-term happiness (up to fifty-seven minutes for me) but can never bring joy, which I have defined (at least financially) as complete satisfaction that you are doing the best you can with what you have. This is good stewardship—it is maximizing the benefit of your income.

When I speak to a Kiwanis Club, I am received no differently pulling up in my several-year-old Lincoln than I would be in a new Mercedes. In fact, the older car probably speaks to my belief in my program. It also underlines for me the fact that I am no longer inappropriately attracted to cars that are bad for my financial future. Once you retrain yourself, cars are the easiest area to save money in. If I "rocket" in any area of spending, it would be books, seminars, and perhaps fine coffee. I am sitting by the fireplace at Panera tapping away on my laptop as I write these words. The coffee is great and the overhead is low. As for my $200-a-month online book-buying habit, I am working through a twelve-step program at the Columbus Metropolitan Library, and last month I spent less than $100.

> *Once you retrain yourself, cars are the easiest area to save money in.*

I am certainly not against new (expensive) cars; I have bought a few in my time. All I am recommending is that they be an income-appropriate expenditure purchased with the full realization of what else you could have done with that money. I have been working on this book for over two years, so naturally when someone strikes up a conversation with me and asks what I do, the topic of my book comes up. I recently spoke to a newly single real estate agent who said she had just turned forty-five and had zero money set aside for retirement and no prospects of sharing in her ex-husband's retirement. What was she doing in a coffee shop at three in the afternoon? She was waiting for a ride to take her to pick up her shiny new SUV, which was in part funded by her divorce settlement. I wanted to remind her to be sure to remember, during her cat-food years of retirement, how cool she had looked in the SUV. But I didn't, since she seemed so *tempo*-happy.

Refocus and Zoom In

Cutting back on car expenses can be part of an overall strategy to achieve many goals. Some families may decide to redirect what would normally be car payments into paying off the mortgage, saving for education, or funding current education. For my family right now, cars have taken a backseat and are of minor importance. We have refocused and zoomed in on education and retirement. My son, A. C., graduates from high school in 2009 and will begin college; my wife, Nita, will be completing law school in 2008; and my daughter, Paige, will be ready for an expensive private girls' school. Along the way in 2006 and 2007, I should be finishing my master's degree and planning for a doctorate. With the exception of law school, most of the above will not cost more per month than two cars. Suppose you are a well-educated family. You have the option of spending a little over $800 a month ($10,000 per year) on two nice cars or you and your wife can complete graduate degrees that would likely double your incomes in five years. What do you do? If you take the two-new-cars route, what are they worth after five years?

Car Math

Suppose you decide that you can get by without a car payment or with a smaller car payment. What do you do with that extra money? Buy a boat? What do you think? Since I can't make a little hand pop out of this book and slap you, let's just look at the math. Suppose you could redirect the $383 a month to a retirement fund for an extended period of time—let's say ten years (120 months)—that could make 9 percent instead of costing you 9 percent. What is the result of our car (or anticar) savings account? After ten years it is starting to look pretty good. I have also thrown in the math for three, four, five, and six years. These seem to be the average lengths of car loans. I have even included the results of forty-year obedience for younger readers.

Number of Months	Return Rate*	Payment	Future Value
36	9%	$383	$15,761
48	9%	$383	$22,030
60	9%	$383	$28,887
72	9%	$383	$36,383
120 (10 years)	9%	$383	$74,115
480 (40 years)	9%	$383	$1,792,946*

* The assumption of a 9 percent return could be based on something simple like a Russell Index Mutual Fund. The gain will come not by your brilliance in picking stocks but with obedience and time. The fact is that the stock market over seventy-five years has averaged more than 10 percent per year return. A Russell-type index fund gives you a piece of the top two thousand stocks on the exchange. I don't recommend any specific fund. If you do not have the ability to safely invest your initial capital, I'd consider these types of funds. From 1926 to 2001, the average compound rate for the S&P 500 Index was 10.7 percent. Source: Professor Roger G. Ibbotson, *Stocks, Bonds, Bills, and Inflation Yearbook* (Chicago: Ibbotson Associates, 2002).

Car Sick?

If you are in debt or just wanting to do something smarter with your money—recall the simple solution to transportation—buy less and drive it longer. Most Americans take great pride in what they drive. Many consumers start itching for a new car before scratching the old loan. Most of us with the "new-car itch" probably don't really need a new car. After a series of constant trading and adding the negative equity from your last car into a loan for the new one (that's what a dealer's ad saying, "We'll pay off your trade," means), consumers find themselves deeper in debt than ever before. If you can "drive out" your mistake (that is, continue to drive it until it is paid for or longer), at least it won't compound on you. Please understand that car dealers aren't there to help you; it is commerce. Like politicians, car dealers cannot give anything to you that they have not first taken from you.

> *Many consumers start itching for a new car before scratching the old loan.*

Transportation is an important place to show restraint. It is probably one of the easiest areas of spending to quickly change. The difference between $259 a month and the average $383 or $447 a month doesn't seem like much over the short term. Yet if you stretch this difference out over thirty or forty years, it is huge, as the examples above illustrate. I was in the real estate business for over twenty years. I have seen many situations where young couples could not qualify for a home mortgage because of one or more car payments. Mortgage loan applications do not have a blank to fill in about the age and mileage on your old car. Lenders are concerned with how much you owe monthly, not how cool you look as you ride. They do not care if the paint on the car is faded. They do need to know if your ability to repay is faded.

The Two-Income Family

My wife and I consciously decided not to compete for a home in a top public school district. When it was time for my son to begin school, we had already opted to continue driving the vehicles we had. This made it easier to pay for A. C.'s private school. We had friends who put their daughter in the same school, but after a time and the purchase of two new cars they withdrew her and she entered the local public school. We never asked if the car payments were the reason, but the correlation and timing seemed pretty clear.

If you can suffer the indignity of pulling up to your child's school in a six-year-old minivan with 156,000 miles on it, you probably can afford private or parochial schools for your children. It's a choice—nothing more. You are pro-choice, aren't you? The lessons our children observe by watching how we handle our finances may ultimately be more important than the school we get them into. Buying two- or three-year-old cars for cash or very low payments allows you to redirect your income to education or savings.

The cost of private school is a long-term investment in the child's future. Think in terms of twelve to sixteen years. The cost of competing for housing in the hot areas of your region to get into a school district where the parents approve of castration by taxation may last longer than twelve to sixteen years. Not only will you pay 25 to 40 percent more for the privilege of living near the supposed best public school; your ongoing taxes are normally 25 to 40 percent higher than in many nearby areas. Don't forget, even if the tax rate is not that much higher, it will cause a dramatic increase in your annual taxes because the county assesses the property at a higher value. It may be the same quality house with taxes 20 percent higher than the same house in your old neighborhood.

Learn or Learn Not to Care

It's unlikely that you will become an expert in used cars. Even if you do, such expertise is a very perishable body of knowledge.

Here is some advice you can always count on: new cars always drop in value. I was discussing my infamous Jaguar with Dan Mershon of *Mershon's World of Cars* in Springfield, Ohio. Few people have owned more new and used cars than Dan, as either a hobby or a business. He specializes in collector cars, selling reconditioned or original Corvettes, Camaros, Mustangs, and so on to forty-something guys and gals who should probably be in mutual funds or rental real estate. The C-5 Corvette had just come out at that time and people were paying over sticker to get one. It was ridiculous. I asked Dan about trading my Jaguar for one. I really wanted to just trade my pain for a different shade of misery, I suppose. Dan suggested that I wait a few years and the rush would be over. He said, "If it's a new car, it's going down in price—guaranteed." He was right. In a few years they were common. I still didn't buy one. Right now, they are no big deal—a nice car but no big deal.

What to Buy?

So what are the basics you need to know to survive a used car purchase? Number one is: don't get emotionally attached to a car. Understand that all go down in price, new or used. Many folks advise buying a two-year-old car, saying it has reached its optimum point of depreciation and remaining useful life. That's generally good advice. There may be other factors, though. Maybe a lower-mileage three- or four-year-old car is a better value if remaining useful life is the important criterion.

I once bought a ten-year-old Lincoln Town Car that looked like new. My rationale? I was able to buy it for about $4,600, or 12 percent of its original sticker price. Based on the mileage and what I know about these cars, it had about 50 percent of its useful life remaining. It was cheap enough for me to just write a check and dependable enough to last a long time. It was also a great-looking car. Would this have been a good deal for you? I don't know. I have had about five of these Lincolns and felt comfortable with them. Besides, my close friend Dave owns an auto repair shop. This Lincoln didn't have any serious problems, but it is a comfort to have someone you trust to work on your cars.

If you know very little about used cars, get a friend who does know about them. In many areas of life, where there is opportunity, there is also a chance of financial loss. At a minimum you need a competent mechanic you can pay to check over a used car you are preparing to buy. I have bought hundreds, but I still have Dave look them over in advance. There is a certain percentage of the population that may be better off with an affordable new car. Some people just seem to be magnets for bad car deals.

Not everyone can competently evaluate a used car. I get help to back up what I think I know. An expert can probably tell if a car has been wrecked and put back together. Even more important, was it put back together correctly? A good full-time mechanic will know which cars or trucks have chronic engine or transmission problems. These are best to avoid, of course. When I was buying cars for fun and profit in my youth, I soon learned which cars to never buy and which were desirable. You can learn this too or you can simply hire good help. I have lived through over three hundred purchases and only the Jaguar I discuss in Chapter 2 really caused extreme discomfort.

Value

I always shudder when I read advice along the lines of "Call your bank or the library and ask the staff to look up the value of a used car for you in the National Automobile Dealers Association (N.A.D.A.) or *Blue Book* guide." First, I would not want to base a several-thousand-dollar decision on what bank tellers or library assistants tell me. They may not know how to adjust for condition or mileage and, if they do, it's doubtful that they will take the time to do it.

Another way to value cars is on the Internet. Always operate from a wholesale perspective and add a little if you find the right car. Yes, even if you are from Hardscrabble, you can buy a car wholesale. Look at www.KBB.com, *Kelly Blue Book*. Use the section that gives you dealer trade-in value. This may not be as severe or accurate as the *Black Book* from Hearst Publications that most dealers use, but it is pretty close and definitely a very usable guideline. The *Black Book* is an average of what cars are going for at the "dealer-only" auctions in a particular region. I have a subscription to the *Black Book*. It is expensive ($105 a year in 2004) and covers cars only up to five years old. I was recently using the *Black Book* to price a two-year-old Camry. In most cases the www.KBB.com trade-in value reports were in sync with the *Black Book*. They were all close enough at least. *Kelly Blue Book's* trade-in value section on the Internet seems to be pretty accurate right now. This could change, but currently, of the few places on the Internet to get trade-in values, it's most closely in line with the information most dealers are purchasing from Hearst Publications such as the *Black Book*. I appreciate a realistic price guide rather than a feel-good price that is unattainable when selling and too high when buying.

Color Me Gone

Truly appraising a car is part art and part hard science. For instance, between two cars with equal miles and condition, the car with the better color would be worth a little more. What's the better color? The one you want? Maybe if you are going to drive it forever. In our area, a brown or pale green car is unde-

184 Good Debt, Bad Debt

sirable. I once bought a chocolate brown Lincoln Town Car cheap and no one wanted it—I had to drive it longer than I originally planned.

Nationally what are the best colors? Number one is usually white, just recently edged out by silver. Red, white, and blue are always popular. The trendy colors (turquoise, purple, lime green) are always a risk. Maybe you are saying to yourself, Color? Is he kidding? Think about it. If you don't care about color, make a low offer on a brown car. The seller might take it, since brown cars have fewer lookers than, say, white cars.

I remember an estate sale where an attorney was selling the proverbial little old lady's car with only a few thousand miles on it for a reasonable price. He had lots of lookers but no offers. Why? It was pale green. If I remember the math correctly, the car had a wholesale market value of about $7,000 but after a time sold for $5,200. If it had been one of these colors:

1. Silver
2. White
3. Red
4. Blue
5. Black
6. Gray

it would have sold for $6,500 to my friend who told me about it. In used cars you don't always have a choice of colors. If you are buying new, give resale some thought.

Depreciate Me, Baby

One thing that is nice about the car business is it has some uniformity that many markets do not have. It is harder to come up with a price on a two-door hardtop (house) in Ypsilanti, Michigan, than a price on a 2001 Honda Accord. Should you worry about how much a car depreciates? If you are going to trade or sell in a few years, depreciation is big. Again, there are two sides to the question. Doesn't every punch have a possible counter-punch? I hate depreciation if I am selling; I may love it if I am buying. If you are purchasing a three-year-old car, maybe you prefer the $6,700 Chrysler Sebring Sedan to the $11,300 Honda Accord LX with the same age, miles, and condition. Sure, I like the Honda better, but the question to ask is "Given my current financial goals and direction, do I like the Accord $4,600 more than the Sebring?" Yes, Mr. Honda, we are friends, but are we $4,600 friends?

The question might be "Does $6,700 fit the budget where $11,300 doesn't?" I don't often see people looking out of the window fretting about how much their car is depreciating, not normal people anyway. To recap: depreciation impacts us only when we sell. It probably won't affect the daily drivability of the vehicle. Cars are commodities to be used and sold. The argument about what is a better car has many sides. Do the Florsheim shoes last longer than the Thom McAn shoes? Are they a better buy? It depends on your circumstances. If you have to borrow money to buy the Florsheims, maybe over the years two pairs of Thom McAns are the smarter buy.

The quickest way to get educated about how fast cars depreciate is to sit down with a hot cup of coffee and a leasing guide. An evening by the fireplace with one of these guides should make you wonder why anyone would buy a new car. Even the hallowed Camry and Accord drop almost 50 percent in three years. Look at the residual values of different cars at the end of two-, three-, four-, and five-year leases. These are projections, yet uncannily they seem to be about the wholesale value of the car when the time rolls around. Not only do you pay all the depreciation when you lease; you have agreed in advance to sell the car back to the lease company for the wholesale price. I am not recommending leasing—the purpose of this chapter is to learn about how cars, trucks, and SUVs depreciate.

One lease guide is called *Automotive Lease Guide*. Many banks have their own guides, which are usually based on estimates from this central source. If you know someone who sells and leases cars, he may be willing to let you have an old copy.

How Much a Month? It's Not $23,000, It's $489 a Month.

I think that for many people, if they saved the amount it took to pay cash for the vehicle they suppose they want, when the time came to purchase it they would prefer to keep the cash rather than going ahead with the purchase of the car. I have no research to back up this assumption, but there are lots of data available showing that consumers spend far more when purchasing on credit. Sales representatives for credit card services commonly tell restaurant owners that patrons will spend up to 40 percent more when they can pay by credit card. Even if the 40 percent figure is an exception and not a rule, one thing is certain: generally many of us will spend more when we don't convert the cost to an actual cash outlay.

Remember in Chapter 1 ("The Debt Effects"), where I say, "Credit allows emotions to trump math—stretching our payments long into the future and reducing the 'right-now cost' to a few dollars a month." If we allow a car salesperson or ourselves to position our decision as a $489 decision and not a $23,000 decision, we are being deceived. At the very least you should ask, Does obligating nearly $6,000 a year ($489×12=$5,868) for transportation fit in with my overall plan? Of course, not having a plan makes it easy to blow off this concern. If you earn $50,000 a year, this is probably over 14 percent of your after-tax income. This 14 percent yearly doesn't even include GTO (gas, tires, and oil), insurance, or fuzzy dice. A few quick calls to your insurance agent can tell you if the car you are buying has unusually high repair rates, thereby making the rate you pay for coverage higher.

No Money Down

Car dealers proudly advertise "no money down" as a benefit rather than the detriment it usually is. Salespeople are trained to sell a monthly payment. Regrettably, a large portion of the public goes along with this. Salespeople are trained to reduce an objection to the ridiculous. Hence, we are told that the deluxe Aardvark 3000 is only $23 a month more—not $1,500 more—than the Aardvark 2000. Is no money down a bad thing? No. It is neither good nor bad. The overall price of the car determines whether it is good or bad. No money down is a function of financing—not value. It has little to do with the car deal itself. It is hard for most folks to keep the two separate, but if you don't, you are falling for the classic scheme for selling cars: you forget the price and concentrate on the payment. This is exactly what the car dealer desires for you.

Preapproved Financing and Prespent Emotions

The best way to keep price and payment separate is to make sure that they are totally separate. If you must finance a car, arrange your financing ahead of time with your bank or local credit union. Do the research about what you will pay for the car before you get to the dealer. This is what I call prespent emotions. Do all of your fantasizing about the car before you go to buy it. This will give you time to realize that it's just another car and to recall that your financial goals are more important than a car. If you don't prespend your emotions before you get to the dealer, you may react to a counteroffer or agree to something you didn't really want. With the emotions gone (or in check at least), you can safely walk into the battlefield of buying a car. Few amateurs emerge unscathed. Most injuries occur because the buyer thinks that he needs to buy now, he wants to buy now, and he's mesmerized by the thought of a shiny new car. You have the ultimate weapon, though. Nancy Reagan taught you, "Just say no!"

Make your offer, be polite, but be ready to walk. If you can't work it out, say, "Let me know if your circumstances change." Then get up and walk. The salesperson will get up and stop you and then go through the typical wailing—"We aren't making any money," "This is the best we can do," "Give me something to work with here," "I'm trying to help you," "You'll never do better elsewhere." He will then go for the T.O. (turnover), hoping that the gold chains and cologne or perfume of the next guy or gal, usually a manager, will break your irrational price resistance.

Where do we risk spending 35 percent a year on something other than a car? Want a new car, a truck, or, for the politically insensitive, maybe an SUV? I can get you one for only 35 percent a year. That is what some people pay for a new car or truck. If you look at leasing guides for residual values, you will see that many depreciate or lose 50 to 55 percent of their value in two years. We have a major car dealer in Columbus that often advertises a current-year popular-model car for $10,900. This car is a little over a year old. It stickers for about $20,000 new and you could buy a new one for about $15,900 to $17,000 as rebates fluctuate every few months.

So how do we get to 35 percent a year in cost? Just add about 25 percent depreciation for the first few years and 9 or 10 percent cost of financing.

Zero Interest—I Have Zero Interest

What about those zero-interest loans? In most cases, I have zero interest in them. Aren't they a good deal? Maybe—in almost all cases you still pay the going rate. If the cost of funds for an average Joe is at 9 percent, that is near the rate you will pay one way or another. If you take the special zero-percent financing, you won't get the reduction in cost or the rebates. These sales incentives are a choice of one or the other—you don't get both. The typical offer is to get $2,000 to $4,000 as a discount or zero-interest financing. You will notice that the zero-interest rates are through the manufacturer's finance division. The main thing to remember on zero-interest loans is that generally any interest not paid is included in the cost of the vehicle.

I have an example: Joe Debtor goes to the local new-car dealer to buy a new Meta Slug XL2. The price of the car is $23,484. Joe has the choice of getting a rebate of $3,000 or a zero-interest loan for forty-eight months.

Number of months (N)	Interest Rate	PMT	Loan Amount (PV)
48	6.9%	$489.57	$20,484
48	0%	$489.25	$23,484

Here Joe may be better off to borrow the money from his credit union or bank at 6.9 percent. Whether this is a vehicle you should buy at all is another story. With a little research you find almost two-year-old Meta Slugs for about $12,900. I want you to set aside the glee words *zero interest* and see that you really are paying for the privilege of telling your friends that you got one of those great zero-interest "deals."

When you are offered zero interest, generally you will want to take the discount in lieu of the special financing. But in each case, do the math and weigh the benefits. Consider a two-year-old car of the same brand. If you are concentrating on the payment, let's look at what would happen if you paid off early. In an early payoff on a zero-interest loan, the manufacturer/lender is the big winner. Because the cost of financing for forty-eight or sixty months is included in the cost of the vehicle, in an early payoff the company earns interest on the entire loan. If you think you may pay off or trade your chariot before the end of the loan, you would probably be better off to have a simple interest loan, remembering that you start your balance at $2,000 to $4,000 dollars less.

I have seen times when a consumer is offered a big rebate or special financing and then in the heat of the moment forgets to negotiate the price. Regardless of the rebates or other offers, the margin of markup on the car remains the same. Often people are so happy to get the $2,000 rebate that they do not ask for any discount on the vehicle. In the particular instance I am thinking about, the vehicle had an additional markup of $2,600 of which a large portion would have been available to the buyer for the asking. He did not ask.

If you need to know the markup in a new car, go to www.kbb.com or www.kellybluebook.com. Just follow the menus and add the options you want. With a little investigation and simple math, you might discover that for a new Ford truck the markup on the base price is 10 percent and on options about 13 percent. Therefore a new Ford Super Duty truck with an MSRP of $29,960 may have an invoice cost of $25,640.

The $8 Million Corvette

"Sherman, set the way-back machine to Columbus, Ohio, 1982."

"Gosh, Mr. Peabody, where are we going?"

"Sherman, we are going to the land of Advice Given, but Barely Taken."

Near the end of 2003, I visited with a financially successful friend of mine named Dan. He asked about how the manuscript for *Good Debt, Bad Debt* was coming. As we discussed it, he asked if certain things were in the book. Most of the things he asked I could answer affirmatively.

Dan said, "The one thing you said at a seminar over twenty years ago that I have never been able to forget is the story of the $8 million Corvette." He then recalled for me my words, making me wish I'd attended and listened rather than taught the seminar. Here are the three points of the seminar as Dan recalled:

1. Don't buy depreciating assets.
2. Don't eat your seed corn. (Dan is from Ross County, Ohio, and he means capital.)
3. Remember future value and the story of the $8 million Corvette.

Apparently, I used as an example a story of how much a $23,000 Corvette (in 1982) would cost a twenty-two-year-old at age sixty-five in terms of lost opportunity costs. I was really parroting an example Jimmy Napier had used earlier in the year. I used the then current assumptions that sound incredible based on today's market interest rates. But at that time (1982) you could earn 14 percent just by putting your money in a bank. So those investing in private mortgage paper were doing better than 20 percent or more.

Certainly it is stretching a most difficult-to-obtain truth. As most politicians know, if you torture the numbers long enough, they'll confess to anything. But strive with me here for a moment. Suppose you could invest $23,000 of capital and earn

13.79 percent for forty-three consecutive years without withdrawing anything. It is true that you would have over $8 million. This is an example that has stayed with my friend Dan for over twenty years.

Months	Return Rate	PMT	Present Value	Future Amount (Future Value)
516	13.79%	0	$23,000	$8,361,406.58

The point of this chapter is to make sure that you make conscious decisions regarding your car expenditures. Do you have a car or transportation expense that is taking you nearer to or farther from your goals? Saving $250 or $500 a month on car expenses may not be too exciting in the beginning, but once you have accumulated some savings, you can watch your net worth grow monthly from investments you direct. Again, the important part is starting and sticking to a plan.

> *They made a decision to watch their net worth grow instead of changing the scenery in their driveway every year or two.*

After the seminar, Dan and his wife, Tracy, did something unprecedented. They verified the math and took action—or, in this case, inaction. They never allowed themselves to be swept away emotionally by new cars. They made a decision to watch their net worth grow instead of changing the scenery in their driveway every year or two. Even though they are now financially able to pay for any car they desire, they continue to prefer two-year-old cars and trucks. Once watching their net worth rise became more pleasurable than feeding the urge for consumer baubles and trinkets, the rest was easy. Their story is pretty consistent with those of couples surveyed by Thomas Stanley and William Danko in *The Millionaire Next Door* and Stanley's *The Millionaire Mind.*

As you do your monthly tracking and tabulation, it is your choice whether you get to add to the positive side of the balance sheet or watch (as average Americans do) nearly $5,000 a year be consumed in burn rate.

Points to Ponder

- Buy less; drive it longer. Invest the difference.
- Do your research before you enter the battlefield of either dealers or private owners. If you don't know what you are doing, find an objective party without an interest in the sale who can help you.
- The average car depreciates at $250 per month. This is the $250 that can make the difference between cat food and caviar in retirement.
- Dump the pride issues. This is about your future.
- Learn to "Just say no!"
- Do not allow yourself to be swept away emotionally by new cars. Make a decision to watch your net worth grow instead of changing the scenery in your driveway every year or two.
- Cars are commodities to be used, not investments.

Chapter Nine
Do I Have Records?
My Pulse Began to Quicken

May I have a receipt for that?

Kadel

The ten-second lesson: "He that despiseth little things shall perish little by little." —Solomon

What would life be without arithmetic, but a scene of horrors? —Sydney Smith

The easiest way to handle bad debt is to deny its very existence. Some of us practice politically correct record keeping— we do not really want to know the truth. When we track and tabulate each expenditure and have the courage to look at the results each month, we have accurate information to work from, which is critical if we wish to improve. —Jon Hanson

Unless you are part of a sadistic experiment to train forensic accountants, you will need accurate records. Poor record keeping will cost you money. This is an irrefutable fact. It has cost me dearly time and time again. When it comes to record keeping, my record is as pure as the driven slush. Napoleon Hill, writing on failure in his 1928 *The Law of Success*, says, "Defeat often talks to us in a 'dumb language' that we do not understand. If this were not true, we would not make the same mistakes over and over again without profiting by the lessons that they might teach us. If it were not true, we would observe more closely the mistakes which other people make and profit by them."

When met with failure, do you immediately go to the source of the problem or do you, like so many of us, say, "It just wasn't my time," "My luck is bad," or "Oh well, better luck next time"? The average man considers every possible reason for failure except his own actions. As I write, it occurs to me how many times, though my stated purpose was to be exceptional, I took the average approach—especially toward the subject of record keeping.

Good and Bad Debt Tracking

How often have you been excited about record keeping? For me, I can truthfully answer, almost never. Does it ever feel like your happiness is just stolen moments between billing cycles? If you will do for ten years what most people will never do, you can do for the rest of your life whatever you wish to do. I often refer to record keeping as tracking and tabulating. If you track and tabulate expenditures, you will soon have a good idea of where all of your money is going. Additionally, you won't need to become a forensic accountant each spring, when it is time to deal with your partner, the IRS. One other reason to track your expenses for good and bad debt is to watch the growth of income on your investments that depend on good debt. For example, if you have a rental house and it has a loan of $75,000, each month you log the cash flow from the property, and the principle pay-down is added to your net worth. Conversely, if you have a lot of bad debt, you see the effect of that and begin to pare it down.

> *The truth I have found is that accurate record keeping will increase your creative ability, not decrease it.*

Until just recently I have always rationalized that the time it takes to keep detailed records and organized plans would take me away from my creative thought processes. I have always valued my creative thinking and writing as far more time-worthy than record keeping could ever be.

The truth I have found is that accurate record keeping will increase your creative ability, not decrease it. How can this be? It's because with accurate records, you give a measure of validity to planning and forecasting. A dose of reality can be a sobering pill, but without it you are merely building castles in the sky (or on paper).

To many, I suppose, this discussion of record keeping seems too elementary. But I assure you that a large portion of the population has little more than a guess of where all of their income is going. I hear it every day: "Where does all my money go?" Certainly those asking pose it as a rhetorical question. The answer probably never really sinks in.

Sloppy record keeping can cost individuals and companies hugely. The costs may come in the form of not claiming a tax deduction, paying a late fee, or losing an opportunity because you don't know your financial status, or just in pure frustration. Along this line record keeping can mean more than just tracking the dollars. Recently I was looking for a survey for a piece of land to resell and could not find it. This not only caused a delay; I ultimately lost the sale.

Ben, wouldn't it be easier to just use
Quicken and a Zip drive?

Detailed Record Keeping?

How detailed do you need your records to be? That depends. I'd recommend total accuracy; a little sin begets a bigger sin. Sins of omission lead to sins of commission. You won't see the problem coming either—record keeping sins can grow by inaction as well as thoughtless action. For me, any sloppiness I allow tends to grow.

My Grandma Hanson was an extreme record keeper. It was said that she had a journal and could tell down to the penny what it had cost to run her household over the years. She came up through the Great Depression, so she knew the value of a penny and having everything accounted for. A favorite family story was how Grandma Hanson would get up every morning, read the obituaries, and then cross the deceaseds' names out of the phone book. Now that's detailed. Is it anal-retentive? Yes. Is it accurate? Yes, deadly accurate.

Perhaps you won't need the detail Grandma Hanson kept, but this is an area where most of us fall down. The Record Keeping Marines are looking for a few good men and women, the mundane, the mindless, the bean counters. Track and tabulate. Are you ready?

Is it ever fun? I asked that question of one of my anal-retentive friends and he said, "I suppose when you see your net worth and income rise to the desired level, it could be considered fun." Do you need a $50 program to keep track of your records? Not necessarily. You can do it by hand, but most people will find that they spend a lot more than $50 worth of time doing it by hand and that's just in the setup stage. If you are inclined to love being on the computer, you will find it neat to download all of your checking account results from your financial institution. Quicken will automatically mark the checks that have cleared.

Using Quicken

I recommend a program called Quicken Home and Business software. Read all about it at www.quicken.com. It's a great site with many valuable links. I mentioned this to someone the other day and he said, "Oh yeah, Quicken, the electronic checkbook." Well yes, if that's all you want. But it will do so much more.

The "checkbook" comment reminded me of the old radio commercial where a guy takes a chain saw back to the store where he purchased it. He tells the clerk at the counter, "When I bought this saw, you promised me I could cut fifteen trees a day! No matter how hard I try, I can only cut two!" The clerk says, "Well, let's have a quick look at it." He pulls the cord a few times and the saw starts with a roar. Over the exhaust of the saw the customer screams, "What's that noise?"

Many people, like the chain-saw customer, may just be unaware of all the abilities of a program such as Quicken. If you'd like to increase your output from two to fifteen "trees" a day, get Quicken or other similar software.

The path I am about to recommend caused me to think of the cartoon you see in this chapter of the man flipping a quarter in the career-challenged individual's hat. (If you were born before 1970, I mean bum. *Career-challenged* is simply the politically correct term.)

Begin using Quicken and within a few months you can easily have a very good picture of where every penny of your money goes. If you think that this is overkill, consider the small drip in your basement. No, not the teenage boy living there, but a small leak in a water pipe that can cause hundreds of dollars in extra expense over a year. Inefficient record keeping is like that dripping pipe. It may only just keep dripping and drain you slowly, or the leak may spring full force and cost you a bundle. How healthy could you be with a little internal bleeding? Not too healthy, right? It's the same way with money.

Hire a Record Keeper?

Even if you hire someone to do your record keeping, you will still need to supply accurate records to him or her. In many respects it's like asking someone to help you blow your nose—you still have to do most of the work and you are responsible for any mishaps. I would hire someone for serious record keeping and tax advice, of course. But it is better that you do the level of personal record keeping I am talking about here. In the future you might want to hire someone else to do the mundane and the mindless, especially for your business. But hopefully these techniques will become lifelong habits for you, at least as far as keeping track of your personal records is concerned.

This is an innovation for me and I don't think that you could delegate the personal details very easily. Besides, it only takes minutes a day to keep updated once you have set up the system. In the future you will be able to delegate and direct better that which you personally know. I would assume that a coach who used to be a player would be better than one who had only read a book about playing football.

When I told a friend that I was working on the record keeping chapter for my book, he gave a knowing grin and said, "Isn't that kind of like having Jeffrey Dahmer write on catering?" I laughed because it was both true and funny. I could regale you with stories of self-inflicted wounds or overpayments and other waste just because of my poor records. In the record keeping hall of shame, I am chief sinner. The good news is that record keeping salvation is available for all who will confess, repent, accept responsibility, and put in the effort to keep the records. Amen.

I Don't Want to Know

Perhaps you fall into the category of folks who would rather not know exactly where they are financially. I myself have been there before. Your instincts may be good; perhaps you are in trouble, but a few of you may find that you are in better shape than you thought.

If you have economic cancer of the bone, wouldn't it be better to know? Say yes! The earlier you detect something like this, the better the chance for remission or even full recovery. Most of us need a transplant, not of economic marrow, but of economic thinking. Throughout this book I have tried to deal mostly with the psychological aspects of being in debt, and there are many to be sure. Denial or delusion is not only unhealthy—it can be financially devastating. Find out where you are financially. But now it's time for your comprehensive checkup. Ready?

Looks like another case of "feng shui record keeping."

The Debt Devil Is in the Details

You might be surprised to see how much the little things in life add up. Remember the epigraph at the beginning of this chapter: "He that despiseth little things shall perish little by little."

The best way to gain perspective, or at least avoid that sinking feeling like the one you get seeing your brother-in-law and his family pull in the driveway unannounced, is to put it all on paper. Quicken provides proper paper perspective. If you put it all in Quicken, you can generate reports and even cool pie charts showing where the money went. I know that many of you are saying, "I really love those pie charts," aren't you? Without good records in an audit or financial planning, you will experience reverse déjà vu. You will be saying to yourself, None of this looks familiar.

If you really need a conversation starter, slide a Quicken pie chart in front of your wife and explain that she has spent 11.4 percent more at the beauty shop thus far this year than during the same period last year, without a corresponding increase in beauty (wait until dinner is over, unless you aren't hungry).

OK, let's talk about how simple this can be. And remember you are hearing from a guy who once felt that viewing his personal record keeping was like taking a tour of a sewage plant in a glass-bottomed boat. It will require a commitment on your part of a few hours to set everything up initially and then an unwavering twenty minutes or less a day. Did I say unwavering?

No, Really, Don't Lie to Yourself

Could you spend twenty minutes a day on this? I didn't hear you? Don't just grunt. Think to yourself, Sure, and read on. Pause and think about it. This is not as easy as it seems. Consider this commitment seriously, with more than the solemnity generally reserved only for New Year's resolutions. By the way, how are you doing on those? Do you exercise for fifteen minutes a day, every day? If you do, that's great. When I get the urge to exercise, I lie down until it goes away.

So if this is just an "I'll try to do it" scenario, you are wasting your time. The Debt Devil loves to hear "I'll try," because he knows this victim is not sold. "I'll try," means "I won't." Brian Tracy says, " 'I'll try' is excusing failure in advance." Your mind will pursue your true inner dialog, not your vain words. Without commitment, there can be no healing.

As I have said in several chapters the learning of the discipline is the key.

Dan's Plan

I recommend my friend Dan's bookkeeping method. He collects receipts every day and the next morning (being a morning person) he sits down and in about five to fifteen minutes has all of his entry work done (he actually uses Microsoft Money). You could do this at night—the key is to develop a habit of doing it. It is easier to do it if you have a regular schedule. Perhaps you can view e-mails, delete spam, open Quicken, enter receipts, and download activity in your bank account in twenty minutes or less. This is, of course, after you take the time and effort to set up the files in the beginning. If you are a Quicken expert, I'd love to hear about how you use the program. My contact information is in the back of this book. At the very least, shoebox all of your receipts and do them all before you go anywhere on your day off. Find a system that works for you. Few will have the discipline that my friend Dan has.

I wouldn't write about this as if it's such a big deal (it is), but if you could call Dan right now, he could look up how much he spent at Kinko's for photocopies in July 1996. Over the years I have done a few real estate deals with Dan and I always have him do the record keeping. When we settle up (sell the asset), he gives me a report with every item delineated down to courthouse parking and the last seven-cent copy. Perhaps I exaggerate just a bit, but I need you to embrace the concept.

Use Dan's plan and within 30 days you will have a solid picture of where your money is going. Within 90 to 180 days all of the quarterly large expenses should have gone through a cycle. If you follow this plan for a year, you will be able to use your reports for budgeting and forecasting expenses.

Why is this so important? Because most people make plenty of money, but they just send it—voluntarily or not—to the wrong places. With accurate records you will be more powerful, since you'll have the information at hand.

If you make $48,000 a year and are able to invest $5,000 a year, you are far better off than Doctor Lotta Bucks making $273,000 a year and saving or investing nothing. It is not the amount you make; it is the amount you do something wise with. Wealth is not about income; it's about accumulation and investment.

Flying VFR in an IFR World

Remember your purpose. Why have you come this far? Was it to implement your plan or settle for mediocrity? By now the Debt Devil is probably whispering in your ear, "You don't want to be a bean counter, do you?" I assure you that this is a worthwhile endeavor. Without good records, you are flying with no fixed point of reference. Without a fixed point of reference, you are like a guy in a small plane who never really knows if his altimeter is correct. If you don't know how high above sea level you are and the terrain in front of you is higher—well, you get the point. Yet many people fly daily without instruments. Flying VFR (visual flight rules) is great when the skies are clear and you can see the whole terrain.

If you are using Quicken or a program like it, you can have the best of both worlds. Fly VFR with IFR (instrument flight rules) to back you up. A financial fog can roll in very quickly!

The worst thing you can do is to be flying VFR in IFR weather. Get instruments; get Quicken or a similar record keeping product.

A Sinking Fund or a Sinking Feeling?

Another area that you can track in your record keeping system is expected expenses. In real estate, we sometimes call this a sinking fund. It's pretty simple: if you know that an expense of $300 has to be paid every six months, you set aside $50 a month in anticipation of the payment. I have a friend who, although he doesn't have a car payment, has a sinking fund to replace his cars when the time comes. In the meantime his car investment (aside from massive depreciation) doesn't cost; it pays.

Budgets

I am not a huge fan of slavish budgets. I know many authors would not dream of telling you not to prepare a budget. Don't start with a budget; start with an actual tabulation of what you are currently spending. You will need a budget for forecasting likely expenses, but it is your goals and desires that keep spending in line. You know the big stuff: rent or mortgage, transportation, insurance, and so on. The problem is probably in the petty cash leakage. It's easy to saw through $300 to $600 or $1,000 a month in small, insignificant things. The preceding numbers are based only on $10 to $34 a day. Whether in cash or charge, it adds up if you are looking for retirement or special project money. What I call petty cash leakage David Bach, author of *Finish Rich*, calls the Latte Factor: money that you just spend but really don't think about. It can add up to a fortune over time as I outlined in Chapter 6 ("What If You Live?").

Once you have a few months of expenses in your record system, you will automatically have a budget. It may not be a good one, but it will be an actual budget, not a budget of where you *think* you are. From there you will be able to see where you can improve. If you do a ninety-day tabulation of actual spending and look at it in total, you will be able to make a livable budget from there. Working from actual spending is less frustrating than working from what you think you should be spending. I think it's easier to bend from where you are than move totally. If you have a spending and saving plan, everything else should follow.

Render unto Caesar . . .

While we are on the subject of record keeping, we might as well address the next requirement, taxes. As Jesus put it, "Render unto Caesar the things which are Caesar's." Yes, you have to keep records, and with Quicken Home and Business, you can have most of the work done and download or transfer it directly into TurboTax. I have used TurboTax since the early '90s. Actually I began with MacInTax, the Macintosh version of the program.

Usually I have a CPA review the results. This helps the CPA timewise and usually he agrees with the TurboTax findings. Also, he charges me a low flat fee just for the work he actually does.

Using TurboTax

If you have never used this program, it will interview you (that is, ask you questions). At first, it asks about all basic stuff: name, social security number, and so on. It simply takes the information and puts it in the correct boxes on the IRS forms. Later it will ask if you had any rental properties for the year, did you pay child care, and do you have a small business?

It even covers some of the more esoteric provisions of the tax code, like fuel credits. When you enter a depreciation schedule for a truck, TurboTax asks if it is over six thousand pounds GVW. The truck question decides whether you can write off $22,000 or more that year or a fraction of that. Perhaps this part of the tax code has helped increase the popularity of the large SUV. If you are in business, the big SUV may look pretty good when you get to deduct over $20,000 of its cost from your gross income, especially when the deduction for a regular car may be only a few thousand. This is not to say that an expensive SUV is a good idea for you. I would not recommend buying an expensive vehicle to avoid paying tax, especially if you run into debt to acquire said vehicle. The payments are sure to last longer than the benefit of any tax savings. Please don't forget that used vehicles get the same tax treatment as new vehicles.

TurboTax is a whiz at some of the semicomplicated forms, like schedules SE, E, and K1 and the depreciation schedules. You type in the answer or the number and, without moaning, TurboTax does the work.

Every year my friend Dave takes his tax preparation to a CPA, who takes all his information and gives it to an employee to do what? You guessed it: enter the information into the professional version of TurboTax.

Who's Responsible? You or Your CPA?

If you fill in the boxes correctly, TurboTax is more consistent and accurate than the pencil-chewing little guy I formerly used. And here's a news flash for you: no matter whose name—even Mr. Big-Time, CPA—is on the bottom of your return, in the event of an audit, it is your body part in the IRS audit wringer, not your CPA's.

I had one of those "guaranteed we will back you up in case of an audit" CPAs. I was audited. What happened? Like a good politician he backed me up—with one hand on the door and the other on my wallet. The fine print says that CPAs will fight for you with your money. Maybe they aren't all that way, but that was my experience.

If you have a good relationship with a CPA, keep it. If you don't, you will need to develop one. Do not be so naive as to think that an inexpensive piece of software will replace the guidance of an experienced CPA. At least with Quicken, you will have your information available at your fingertips, which alone should save billable hours from your CPA.

You will feel a certain sense of accomplishment by just having all of your finances accounted for. Whether you use the system I recommend here is up to you. After a long period of trial and terror, I recommend what I think is realistic for most people.

I do have friends who keep all of their records in shoeboxes, in double-ledger entry books, and in a number of other places. The cartoon of Ben on page 197 shows how I imagined his basement storage system. His grandfather taught him to never throw anything away. The system seems to work for Ben and gave me an idea for the cartoon, but it seems a little cumbersome to me.

It Will Never Last

I remember thinking that nail guns in construction were a fad. Now everyone in construction uses them. Not only do they increase productivity; they can do a few things you can't do by hand. For instance, if you are nailing new work to an existing wall with a nail gun, the nails pop in quickly without shocking and disturbing the nails and tape on the existing wall. If you do it the old way—shock the nails in with a thirty-two-ounce hammer—you will likely damage the drywall. The same is true for some computer applications over the old-school way. Not only are these applications quicker and more accurate, but with a program like Quicken you can generate reports and comparisons you would never even conceive of doing by hand.

SYSTEM: Save Yourself Time, Energy, and Money

If you haven't caught my drift yet, get some type of system. It has often been said that **system** is an acronym for **s**ave **y**ourself **t**ime, **e**nergy, and **m**oney. This idea comes from Mark Victor Hansen and Robert Allen's book *One Minute Millionaire* and program of the same name. Everyone should have a system. Whatever your system is, make sure that it can catch everything down to the quarter you flip into the bum's hat.

Points to Ponder

- Tabulation beats speculation as to where the money went.
- Set a system up to catch all of your spending.
- You have a partner, the IRS. Deal it in, and plan for the yearly event.
- You might be very surprised at how much you spend on take-out food or in many other seemingly insignificant areas.
- Set a sinking fund for recurring expenses, be they quarterly, semiannual, or annual.
- Only with accurate accounting can you safely increase and monitor your net worth and cash flow.
- Tracking and tabulation are critical to wealth metrics as discussed in Chapter 6 ("What If You Live?").
- Your core desire to be successful will outlast and outperform any budget or list of goals you make. When you know why, how, and what "success" will mean to you, this is your most powerful tool. Your "why" must be bigger than your "how."

Chapter Ten
You Married Who?
The Ultimate Good Debt—Maybe

Honey? Aren't you going to help me with my bags?

The ten-second lesson: "Take the daughter of a good mother."
—Thomas Fuller

Men see themselves as the husbands we know we could be. Women see us as the husbands we actually are.

—Jon Hanson

The first "bad debts" of marriage often come from the ceremony and the reception. It is foolhardy to borrow money to get married.
—Jon Hanson

"Marriage may make or mar your entire life. It can build you up or tear you down. It can ennoble every phase of your character, or it can make you a cringing failure. It is a perilous mistake that so few men or women receive any sort of correct instruction about the problems of married life." So wrote Bernarr MacFadden in his 1937 book *Be Married and Like It*. You might say that marriage imitates a Dickens passage with equal chance of becoming the best of times or the worst of times. Marriage and personal finance require considerable research, forethought, and planning.

Love, marriage, and money are areas of life that are highly emotionally charged. They almost always begin with an appeal to the heartstrings. If you are able to stand firm during an emotional storm and make your love, marriage, and money decisions while tethered to reason, the long-term benefits can be tremendous. People who let go of the tether and rely on emotion alone will soon find themselves lost and without the aid of reason or sense—and no rope to follow back to reality. A good marriage adds to your life, much like good debt. An ill-conceived marriage, much like bad debt, may drain your emotions daily. Just as your financial statement may be improved, so may your marriage balance sheet. Marriage has a cost in both time and resources. A good marriage creates a dynamic return where the benefits far exceed the costs. A good marriage is your highest-returning good debt.

More than 150 years ago, Henry Taylor wrote in *Notes from Life*, "And marriage being thus the highest stake on this side of the grave, it seems strange that men should be so hasty in the choice of a wife as they sometimes are." If there is an area of life that requires clear, sober thinking and common sense, this is it. Have you ever heard men or women regretting whom they find themselves married to? Some people act as though they had no choice in the matter, as if spouses were government-issued. My dad used to say, "In the Army they told us if Uncle Sam wanted you to have a wife, he would have issued you one!" It is unclear whether government-issued wives would increase the divorce rate above its present level. Currently 50 percent of marriages end in divorce—the other 50 percent end in death.

> *Currently 50 percent of marriages end in divorce—the other 50 percent end in death.*

As to my marriage, twenty-one years is a lot of time to amass regrets—and I can think of none. Nita and I were married on July 2, 1983. Do I ever think of another woman? Of course, I do. I'm married—not dead. When I see a gorgeous female walk by, I notice, but I never imagine my life without Nita. I can honestly say to my wife, Nita, "I like me best when I am around you." I am one of the blessed few that married their trophy wife in their youth.

Comedian and philosopher Alan King once quipped, "If you want to read about love and marriage, you'll have to buy two books."

Ben Franklin said, "Fools rush in where angels fear to wed."

Then there's the old maxim "Love is a delusion easily cured by marriage."

Alistair Begg says, "Every man should have a wife if only to keep him humble." If you can't find humor in marriage you have either had a lobotomy or never married.

Whom you marry will greatly affect your financial future. I can hear everyone who's married mumbling, "No kidding!" and not only for the most obvious reasons. Yes, there is more to marriage than just financial considerations, but financial problems can be a black cloud over many marriages. How a husband and wife handle their finances is not the only test of character in a marriage—but a very practical one.

As said with elegance by Samuel Smiles in *Character*, "Man's moral character is necessarily powerfully influenced by his wife. A lower nature will drag him down, as a higher nature will lift him up."

A man or woman might be blinded by love, base physical attraction, family or friends, or any number of wrong influences, and make an emotional decision to marry a ne'er-do-well. And with restrained sarcasm I might add that you will find that some people, whether male or female, are less than honest at the beginning of a relationship.

Financial Infidelity

Marriage counselors tell us that the number one cause of conflict in marriage—even more than issues of personality and kindness—is finances. An often-quoted statistic says that 80 percent of divorces are a direct result of financial difficulties. Selfishness and an unwillingness to defer gratification are at the root of most marital spending problems. And if money already spent is not enough to argue about, just pile on a big old stack of debt!

Debt, together with poor spending habits, can focus the marriage on financial infidelity with monthly reminders (bills) of your indiscretions at a time when you and your spouse should be growing and planning for the future. If you do not have a spending plan in place, you or your lovely spouse will be more likely to slip away for a financial quickie involving money earmarked for savings or even the basic necessities. Once the trust is broken, often the other spouse escalates the problem with retaliatory spending. If Ima Debtor gets a new rug for the hallway, why shouldn't Joe Debtor have the eighteen-volt DeWalt cordless power tool pack? Charge it, please.

Pray, Plan, and Act

If you are already married and struggling, what should you do? If you feel that you need to change the direction of your marriage, it may be difficult. Both parties must agree to change. I don't mean that each of you should agree that the other needs to change. Perhaps you can be the bigger (more mature) spouse and make the good-faith move of positive change alone, at first. If you are a person of faith, pray. If you are otherwise, *plan.* Personally, I find that combining both is the best. To both prayer and planning, however, you must add action.

If you are not married and want to be, become a student of marriage. What do you mean, "It's too much work?" Remember, 85 percent of the satisfaction you ever know comes from your relationships with others, and the relationship with your spouse is the key.

I would never recommend investing in real estate without careful study and research, nor would I ever recommend marriage without the same careful study and due diligence. Where common kindness, joy, and true love are missing in a marriage, no amount of financial success can compensate. Many people mistakenly think that *things* will make them happy. They won't. Go ahead and try; I'll wait. I had to discover this for myself, too. Is it possible to have everything financially in marriage yet still be miserable?

Flight School

To fly a plane, you need months, maybe years, of flight school and ground school together with an aptitude for math and the skill to pilot the plane in many different situations. Currently to get married, you need only a $20 license and a pulse. The ease of getting married reminds me of the youngster telling his grandpa, "Gramps, I've got half a mind to get married." Grandpa replies "Go ahead, son. That's all it takes."

One Plus One Equals One (1+1=1)

Unlike in record keeping, in marriage I speak from a viewpoint of long success. I am not saying that a potential spouse is incapable of being different from his or her parents, but you face an uphill struggle to go against this rule. "Take the daughter of a good mother," is nineteenth-century advice not to be ignored! In marriage math, two become one. In a traditional Christian marriage, two become one in Christ (Christlike thinking that is). Whether Christian or not, the analogy of two becoming one means two distinctly separate people sharing one purpose—not one brain.

Looking back through my journal, I find, "If you do not love your potential mother-in-law, why would you want to marry her offspring?" This doesn't mean that you should have an improper attitude toward your mother- or father-in-law. What it means is you should seek the attributes you want to find in your fiancé in your potential in-laws. It is very likely that they will be duplicated in your spouse. After all, aren't you getting ready to splice a bud off the parents' tree onto yours? Say yes. This advice is especially worthwhile if you intend to have children.

> *The analogy of two becoming one means two distinctly separate people sharing one purpose—not one brain.*

You may win the heart of your prospective spouse, but it's unlikely that you will break the years of training and habits of his or her family. If the family provided good training, then that works to your benefit. I suppose that there are some individuals who live independent of the shadow of their upbringing—but they are rare indeed. Here I need to paraphrase the old real estate maxim, a vacancy is a pleasure compared with a bad tenant. The lesson here could be that being single (a vacancy) is a pleasure compared with having a bad marriage.

You Married Potential?

I have a great wife. I have had more than one person wonder aloud why Nita married me. I don't take offense—I attribute it to prayer, planning, and action. I think that it underscores what a wise choice I made. I used to joke that Nita married me for my potential. But isn't that why couples should select each other—for their potential? We say that we marry for companionship or love, which is true, but we also marry because we feel that marriage will add something to our lives. In my wife I find my lifelong love and my most enthusiastic supporter. Without my wife, Nita, you would not be reading these words.

The Checklist

Is there any one thing you can do to gain clarity before you meet Princess Too-Cute or Prince Charming? Yes! The same thing you should do for every important decision: put it on paper; clarify it in your mind. Once you have reduced what you are looking for to paper, you have a tangible description of desire. That doesn't sound very romantic, does it? When I decided that I wanted to get married, I went to my legal pad and wrote out twenty-six attributes I highly desired in a wife. Some of you might be thinking, Boy, this guy has read too many of those darn positive thinking books! It was while on this self-help high, or near overdose, that I bounced into my normal coffee shop for refreshment and met my wife-to-be.

I believe that it was on the first, but no later than our second, date that I pulled out my legal pad and announced, "This might sound more like a job interview than a date, but would you mind if I asked you a few questions?" Notice how when we're totally focused on a goal, no question seems too crazy? Nita said, "That would be fine." She answered all of the questions satisfactorily and I knew that I had found my girl. We were married within eight months. I have long since lost the pad, but as far as shopping lists go, it was my best.

I talked about my marriage checklist during my real estate seminars in the mid-1980s, while stressing the importance of a checklist for real estate. Invariably several people would come up later and ask for a copy of my marriage checklist. I probably could have sold more copies of that marriage checklist than I did of my first two self-published real estate books: *Selling Sellers* and *Buying Bankless.*

Before I do my best to remember the sum and substance of the list, I must tell you that people laughed, they guffawed, and they said, "No way!" when I shared this story. Why? Well, it is a little uncommon. Having learned that if you always do common things you will have a common life—and not seeking a common life or a common wife—I chose to bring out my list.

At the beginning of this chapter I wrote that marriage is one of the areas of life that are emotionally charged. You could also apply the basic theory from Chapter 2 ("Emotional Hostage"), the Newton-Hanson Theory: "In a financial [marital] transaction, every unbridled emotion has an equal and opposite dulling effect on common sense." As we have learned throughout *Good Debt, Bad Debt,* a key way to bridle or restrain dangerous emotions is to contain them on paper. The first step in changing a thought into a tangible, useful item is to capture it on paper.

My Marriage Checklist

Here is a partial listing of what I discussed with Nita. I eliminated some of the minor items and time has erased others. I offer my list only as an illustration. What is important to me may have little or nothing to do with your list. Perhaps after reading this book, you will want to have a discussion of burn rate, delayed gratification, and retirement. If you are getting married and not thinking forty or fifty years down the road, you are making a big mistake. While considering this list, do not concentrate on what you want—concentrate on what you cannot do without. It's not a wish list. It's a list of deal breakers or "must haves."

SAMPLE MARRIAGE CHECKLIST

1. *Delayed gratification.* Will you be willing to do with less temporarily, to have more down the road?
2. *Houses, cars, and stuff.* We will go through houses, cars, and stuff quickly if it is profitable for our long-term plan. We cannot be emotionally attached to things (I was the first to violate this rule).
3. *Religion.* I wanted a Christian marriage. Update: I knew not what I was asking. This has been harder on me than on Nita. She grew up in the church; I did not.
4. *Support for each other's dreams, even as they evolve.* This has been tough. I tend to think that my dreams are more important than Nita's. Actually, after twenty years, Nita and I both are proceeding rapidly to some of our biggest goals.

For Nita, this means law school; for me, it means writing, speaking, and promoting my books.

5. *Delayed children—maybe forever.* Update: I'm blessed that I have two great children and wouldn't change that for the world. Early on I had decided not to have children. Most of the children I knew, including me, I would not have wanted to reproduce.

6. *Continuing, lifelong education.* We would devote a certain measure of resources to continuing education and seminars. This seems like a small thing in the scheme of things, but whether it's a seminar on marriage, real estate, or publishing, the commitment to lifelong learning has changed our lives dramatically.

7. *Church involvement.* I was pretty poor on this until the children arrived. Again, the foundation and promises I made early on eventually won out.

8. *Independence.* Walk in the opposite direction of the crowd if they are not going your way. It takes a quiet maturity to walk against the crowd. I lost track of this for a few years, getting caught up in residing in just the right neighborhood and following an imaginary reference group.

9. *Time alone.* This was a personal request. I need a few hours each day to write and plan in my journal. I do this best alone. I wanted to know that my wife would not take offense at this. My life is greatly improved when I can have time to think on paper.

10. *Planning summit at least once a year.* This usually involves Nita and me going to a nice hotel (even if it's local), having a nice dinner, and reviewing plans. This is an easy one to drop the ball on also.

But They Look So Nice

Common sense is not a, well, *common* building material used at the beginning of most courtships. Many young men and women remember to shine the shoes, press the suit, and smell lovely, yet they do not dust off common sense to tote along. "Seeing" what they desire, they give little thought to their intended's philosophy of life. We can all think of someone who is a lovely "container" but damaged inside one way or another. I once bought a house with structural problems that were hidden from my sight. The owner had laid up a completely new block wall in front of the cracked and damaged wall to hide the defect. Please remember that sight is only one of the senses you use to select a spouse. Don't forget insight, which is gained through interview and conversation, also known as courtship. As defined, courtship is a time when you must be careful not to oversell or underask.

As defined, courtship is a time when you must be careful not to oversell or underask.

It is vital to have a plan before you look across the table into your potential spouse's eyes. When you take time to discover the values and philosophies of your intended, you may save yourself years of grief. Just ahead I will have a section titled "Conflicting Philosophies." Please give it careful consideration. If you think that marriage is not a financial transaction, you are correct in the strictest sense. It is hopefully about love, respect, and a lifelong companionship that honors God. But to believe that marriage will not affect your financial lifestyle is absolutely insane.

Kevin, you did well for yourself.
Julie, you could have done better.

Conflicting Philosophies

Is it better to know if you have totally different goals and philosophies on life right up front? If you are married to some-one with an incompatible life philosophy, nod your head and say yes! If we are agreed that your philosophy of life is taken from the total of all you know—concentrating on what you think is important enough to guide you—then you must agree that con-flicting philosophies can cause great discord in a marriage. What if one spouse has a philosophy of party-party (if you are old, please note that *party* can now be a verb) and the other has the philosophy of family? Aside from family parties, they don't go together very well, do they?

Many people start a relationship and are afraid that they will offend someone by being themselves. It is unlikely that you can repress your true self for long, so I say let it out soon. Can you imagine all the time and money that would be saved if we were ourselves on a first date? Can you imagine how many more single people there would be?

Why wait until you discover that you can't stand each other? I have a single friend who says, "If there is discord, pull the ripcord!" He may be single forever, since he bails before he pulls out any list. Then there are a couple I know who've been married for years. They have two kids and have decided they disagree on, well, almost everything. They have narrowed down their arguing to just one quarrel: who is the most disappointed. After an evening with these two, I am certain that a duel with pistols would be more humane.

Heard in passing:

Joe: "I expect my wife to be the same twenty years from now as she is today."
George: "That's unreasonable!"
Joe: "That's what she is today."

Newlywed: "Ah, love is grand."
Divorced Guy: "Yeah, about one hundred grand."

Here's another ten-second lesson:

When dating, men and women alike display themselves in the showroom, where everything is quite lovely. The sale is made and everything is fine, until a service or warranty issue arises. Then often we find the sales department has overpromised and the service department will not honor the promises of the salesperson. Perhaps we should ask early, "Will I service what I sell?"

—Jon Hanson

Since some change is inevitable, it is important to make sure that your intended is of sound character and compatible philosophy. If the foundation is cracked or missing, no matter what you build, it will shift and fail.

Fixer-Upper?

If you are the ever-optimistic person who thinks that you can marry someone and change him or her into the perfect mate, don't waste your time. I do not mean to suggest that people cannot change; I have changed a lot. What I am saying is that people will change only if they want to. Every change is subject to the human will trained by its past. Many times, even those who wish to change will be ruled by their past and their egos. Few yield totally to an-

> *Every change is subject to the human will trained by its past.*

other's will, and you wouldn't want to marry someone like that anyway. Find the right person first—a structurally sound person. Save the notion of a "fixer-upper" for houses, cars, businesses, and the like. Bad relationships, especially fixer-uppers, bring a lot of baggage and can take years to unpack.

When you pull out your list, if your date/prospect is offended, then it is more than likely that he or she will be offended by delayed gratification, which was one of the first items on my list (your list will be different). Though a young lady never presented me with a list, I would not rule out the possibility of a female doing this. I'd want my daughter to have such a list if a suitable gentleman did not naturally appear. Perhaps with more tact than I had at twenty-six, you could discover the answers to your questions over a few days. The laserlike focus I employed may not play well with all personalities.

Successful marriage is achieved not by finding a flawless partner, but by finding a highly compatible partner and forgiving each other flawlessly while continuing on the plan you have created for your lives. Where there is true love, small daily kindnesses will preserve and build it.

Get the Big Rocks in First

The "big rocks" idea comes from a sermon I heard a few years ago. A professor was asked to come up with an illustration for a friend who spoke on time management. The professor read his friend's time management book and came up with the following illustration that he presented to his class.

The professor says to his students, "I will take this one-gallon beaker and begin to fill it with materials. You tell me when it is full." The professor takes very large rocks and places them into the clear, glass beaker. He brings the rocks to the top and asks, "Is it full?" A few of the students say yes, but most say it is full of large rocks. The professor then takes smaller gravel and pours it over the big rocks. The gravel trickles down and around the big rocks and then he asks, "Is it full?" All the students say, "Yes, now it is full." Then the professor pours in some fine sand, which slowly works its way down over the rocks and gravel. The beaker appears to be solidly packed. The professor asks, "Is it full now?" Everyone again says, "Yes, it is definitely full now." Then the professor takes a pitcher of water and pours it over the sand, gravel, and big rocks. The container absorbs the entire pitcher of water. He asks, "Is it full now?" They all agree that it is full now! Even the professor says, "Yes, it's pretty full."

Then the professor asks, "If this was to be an illustration of how time management works, what is the moral of this illustration?" A student quickly raises his hand and says, "No matter how full your life is, you can always cram in some more?" The professor laughs heartily and says, "No, the moral of this illustration is that if you don't get the big rocks in first, you will never get them in."

That is why I call the things on my marriage checklist the *big rocks*. The big rocks are the foundation of your philosophy. These are the things that are important to you, generally moral items. Negotiate on these and you will probably have a difficult marriage. Don't think of what you'd like to have—think of what you can't do without.

My Big Rock Parable

A marriage, like a house or any permanent structure, needs a strong foundation. The deeper and wider the foundation, the higher the marriage can safely rise. The marriage foundation is a blending of both spouses' philosophies. Suppose we say that each of our personal philosophies is a big rock. It's best to make sure to have the big rocks in before all the sand and gravel and rain of daily life come washing in. You could say that the sand, gravel, and rain are the daily cares of life. These may include things people outside of your marriage ask of you also. Before you let your beaker fill with these cares, be sure that you and your spouse get your big rocks in.

If you didn't get your big rocks set before you were married, it's not impossible to go back and put them in, but you will have to do a lot of digging and backfilling. Note: you will have to set aside all of the small stuff to get the big rocks in. If you have selected the wrong big rocks, you will have to do major excavating or maybe even blasting—if you and your spouse can even agree on what big rocks should be in there. The simple list I had *before marriage* helped Nita and me agree on the big rocks.

Some couples just walk away from their building site and start another foundation with new building partners. I know a few "contractors" still paying construction fees to their former partners. We see the results of incomplete buildings (marriages) everywhere.

Figure out the big rocks before you send out the engagement announcements; draw up the blueprints together; consult with other successful marriage builders, a marital architect, clergy, or other professionals as needed; observe other successful building sites (functional families); then build the foundation deep, wide, firm, level, and true.

True Confessions

How did I get to be so smart about marriage by age twenty-six? By making many mistakes earlier. Since I shall eventually have to tell my children that I was married and divorced at age eighteen (seven long years before I met their mom), I suppose now is a good time. At eighteen I was married for a total of 351 days. She was an alluring and charming eighteen-year-old girl. With the benefit of hindsight, I know we both were pretty immature. My first wife was a devoted spendthrift and her highest aim in life then was to have a good time. We had no children and parted amicably. I haven't seen her in probably twenty-five years.

Though she had many wonderful qualities, we failed in our marriage because we didn't agree on the big rocks. In fact, I had no big rocks theory at age eighteen. Based on my present understanding of marriage, I cannot say one thing bad about my ex-wife.

Divorce

The old bromide "Two can live as cheaply as one" is probably true—until a couple attempt to set up separate homes. Few things are as devastating financially as divorce, especially if you mix in a few children. Strictly from a financial standpoint, divorce is a bad move generally. I can think of instances where someone gets away from an unfaithful spouse, an addicted gambler, or a drunk, and perhaps projecting those benefits over a just a few years divorce may is the only realistic choice.

Given my Dr. Phil–type attention span, I like what the good doctor said when asked, "When should you get divorced?" Dr. Phil said when you have worked through all of your anger, frustration, and hurt. Wow! That could take awhile, right? I was so impressed by Dr. Phil's answer because that is where I had worked myself to at age eighteen before agreeing to the dissolution of marriage. Early on I had a lot of anger, frustration, and hurt.

I had no special insight or counseling, but I did know that at some point all of the anger, frustration, and hurt had passed. When we agreed to divorce, it was no more emotional than buying a lawnmower to me. Now, I don't want to minimize my ex-wife's importance or feelings here, but I really can't tell you how she felt. It does seem that we both have had better lives apart since that day so long ago.

I know that a lot of guys who get divorced can never find any peace or joy because they have unfinished business with their ex-wives. I cannot speak for women, but by inference I assume that the same is true for them. If you harbor hate or resentment, it will have an effect similar to that of bad debt: you experience loss of freedom, loss of time, and loss of opportunities—maybe even loss of cash flow—so it could be all four of the debt effects. My point is that hate is a wet blanket on your whole life. We know that forgiveness is divine, yet to make your antagonists suffer is more fun. But the fun is shallow and unsatisfying—we must forgive and let go. One of the best books on dealing with anger, frustration, and hurt is *Forgive for Good* by Dr. Fred Luskin. Even if this is not a problem you struggle with, it may give you insight in dealing with others.

My wife says I never listen to her,
or something like that.

Children

Samuel Smiles, in *Home*, observes, "Home is the first and most important school of character. It is there that every human being receives his best moral training, or his worst; for it is there that he imbibes those principles of conduct which endure through manhood, and cease only with life." You are blessed if your parents talked openly about money, spending, and even debt. More than talking, though, if your parents led by example, this has probably had a greater influence on you.

More ten-second lessons:

You can't take your children somewhere you aren't going.
—John Croyle

Our children are messengers we send into a time we will not see.
—Dennis Rainey

If You Dare Reproduce . . .

"The problem with the gene pool is there is no lifeguard!" says funny man Steven Wright. Perhaps there is something to be said for eugenics. For most of us, though, the gene pool is just fine. Many of people's undesirable traits result from faulty training or the environment in which we live. Funny seeing a section on children in a book on debt, isn't it? And you probably think I will blather on about what to spend or not spend on your children. No. That's been done and continues to be done.

What we must be concerned about is the habits you pass on to your children. These should be of more concern than the daily minutiae of what is actually spent. Robert Fulghum said, "Don't worry that your children never listen to you—worry that they are always watching you."

> "*The problem with the gene pool is there is no lifeguard!*"

If you have a past similar to mine, you improve it by a measured combination of the three Es: education, effort, and enterprise. Make no mistake, we need children who can grow up and change the world. But please don't bother having children unless you are willing to raise them and teach them. What this ultimately means is that you will have to be continually learning. Here is what we teach our children: "Never read *over* a word. If you don't understand it, get a dictionary and look it up, without exception." I still do this myself. This was a rule I had to use when I went back to school late in life. We are truly in charge of our own learning. I am glad that I finished college, but most of what I know and use daily comes from reading twenty-five to fifty nonfiction books a year. If you can teach your children to learn, it is the best gift you can give them. In the Preface I talk about how books changed my life; it is no exaggeration. My wife and I are the first in our families to ever obtain bachelor's degrees, let alone the expected doctorate and law degree. Children rarely exceed the educational level of their parents. You may break the trend in your family or help your children break the trend. I had no interest in liberal arts study until I had children to set an example for. It has been a great thing for me, and my son was able to attend my graduation.

> *Example has more recruits than reasoning ever will.*

It has become a popular sport (I play some) to criticize the public education system in America. Yet sometimes as parents we don't give the system much to work with. Learning must start at home.

Example has more recruits than reasoning ever will. Broke and confused parents generally create broke and confused young adults. Your children will do as you do more than as you say. When children hear their parents discuss packing Grandma or Grandpa off to the nursing home, the parents are training their children on how to handle them in later years. The same principle applies to finances.

Daddy, Are We Rich?

What do you say when your ten-year-old asks, "Daddy [or Mommy], are we rich?" Maybe she follows with "Why not?" Do you say, "I planned to fail?" or "I failed to plan"? Or do you shift blame in other ways? "The government. Taxes are too high!" "I wasn't able to go to college." "I was born to a poor family." Any combination of "could have," "would have," or "should have" is insufficient. You can't "should've done" something; you either did or didn't take care of business. It is time to embrace your situation with full frontal clarity—where you are is where you have taken yourself.

It is easy to come up with excuses, but that small voice in your head is always there. It won't let you forget. It was you that chose to skip college and take a "settle-for" job to get a new car and an apartment. It was you who thought $100 a month for cable TV was preferable to a Roth IRA. In fact, you could say that you have been in charge of you all these years. Tell the kid the truth. More important, be truthful to yourself. Aren't you where you're at because of your choices and the ability or inability to delay gratification and control your burn rate? Fun, isn't it? The reason that parents don't like these questions is that we don't like the answers. When the question comes, we know sufficient time has passed. We should be far ahead of where we are financially. The truth is incontrovertible.

Probably the first time as an adult that I broke down and wept like a complete baby was at the birth of my first child. Not because he was hideous to look at, but because I was so overwhelmed by the impending responsibility and the thought that he would be looking to me as a role model. I did what even devout atheists do when the heart squeeze is severe enough—I prayed to God and began to make deals. "God, if you help me with this, I will be a better man. I will go to church. I will . . ." and the list went on.

What Is Really Important in a Family

To gain great wealth and lose your family in the bargain is a poor trade. We have all seen the man or woman who spent all of his or her time on a career while the family grew further and further away. Is any man ever wealthy enough to repurchase his past? No. Not one. Not at any price. Perhaps we could negotiate. "What about very adequate wealth and a slightly dysfunctional family?" No, that is not what I had in mind either.

I'll Have More Time for the Kids When I'm "Rich"

While you are fighting financial alligators, it's hard to remember why you crawled into the swamp. I know a man who is a decamillionaire and I would not trade his net worth for mine if I had to have his family relationships with the deal. The reason why I point this out is that your kids need to see how you became wealthy, rather than just have you show up one day after being missing in action for twenty or thirty years. Children are always watching and listening. But take heart; I have another friend in the same wealth and age range who has excellent family relationships. Both men built successful businesses, one in law and one in real estate; the difference was the care and maintenance of the family relationships. One has joy; one is searching and lost—they both have money.

Of the many men and women who sacrifice family for monetary success, I repeat for effect, can anyone ever repurchase his or her past? There is, of course, the ignorant flip side of this issue, too. Many use family as an excuse to be poor. "If it wasn't for my kids, my wife, my mother, my father, my brother, etc., I'd be rich." Actually, kids and family should offer the best reason to be successful. But better than handing kids the future, as you see it, teach them the skills to be successful on their own.

Points to Ponder

• Love, marriage, and money are areas of life that are emotionally charged. Take the proper precautions to make wise decisions. Apply at least a little more common sense than emotion to your decisions.

- Avoid financial infidelity by working from a spending plan.
- Create and use a big rocks checklist before marrying.
- Example has more recruits than reasoning ever will. If parents model good financial habits, it is likely that their children will apply them. If necessary, be the one in your family who breaks the mold.
- "You can't take your children somewhere you aren't going," said John Croyle.
- A financially healthy marriage will encourage open discussions of spending, saving, investing, borrowing, tax planning, bequeathing, and charitable giving.

Conclusion

Passion costs too much to bestow on every little trifle.
                                                    —Thomas Adams

Failure is God's way of saying, "Excuse me, you are headed in the wrong direction."
                                                    —Oprah Winfrey

If we could build our lives around bumper sticker truisms, the two above would be a good start financially. We spend much of our time, effort, and passion on trifles. We half apply proven methods and then stubbornly decide that they won't work. Some of us throw out the old bucket before seeing if the new bucket will hold water. Each New Year's Day, millions of Americans seek a new bucket and resolve to change their ways, get out of debt, lose weight, or spend more time with friends.

At their core, the concepts of *Good Debt, Bad Debt* are easy to understand but hard to apply. What I have been taking pains to show is that financial success is rather simple, and that daily actions decide the realities of tomorrow. There are few things, aside from health, that affect as many areas of your life as do your finances. Who you are financially determines not only where you live, and maybe even how long you live, but also how many other people you can help in life. Understanding the concepts of the debt effects, emotional management, burn rate, and delayed gratification can change your life. If you understand and apply these principles in your life, you will finish far ahead of the majority of people in this consumption-driven society.

I began in the Preface by telling you that the idea for *Good Debt, Bad Debt* came from wanting to leave a written record for my children. We will all leave a legacy, good or bad, or, as I quipped a few days ago, "He left not so much a legacy as a stain."

It would be hard to believe that we've been put on this earth to live lives of debt, regret, and broken dreams. Yet it is not hard to believe that others would wish us to live in slavery to debt, especially if it gives them power over our lives or enriches them personally. Here is the rub. To whom do we listen? Our consumption-driven culture says, "Shop until you drop. You deserve the best!"

Many seem to follow the consumption-driven plan, leaving this earth with little or nothing as a legacy to either family or charity. Some leave a legacy of debt. That's worse than the father in the Temptations' song: "Papa was a rollin' stone, and when he died, all he left us was alone." I suppose that you could change it to "and when he died all he left us was a loan."

> *Blaming lack of savings on income is like blaming adultery on marriage.*

Once we begin to see that we are falling behind and retirement doesn't look as we thought it would, many fall prey to get-rich-quick schemes. Certainly some people do get rich "quick" but generally it's after a long period of study and effort. It is disingenuous to imagine ourselves millionaires while not even taking steps to first be thousandaires. Remember Longfellow's words, "Most people would succeed in small things if they were not troubled with great ambitions." This is how most of us fail, by ignoring the small things, the simple daily duties of life that are really the building blocks of our greater ambitions.

So, how then shall we proceed? If you are blaming circumstance, government, or other people for your financial status, you need to stop. This robs you of your passion—I know! A few years ago I could have written an entire book on blaming others. It is easy to think, If I made more money, I would have better spending habits. Blaming lack of savings on income is like blaming adultery on marriage.

I have tried to impart one simple message: think! Think about how today's actions will affect what you can do in the future.

> *What to do is simple; carrying it out over twenty years or more is where it is difficult.*

Your financial future needn't be a vague destination when you do what you know is right. What is right? I'd say it is a plan based on sound financial principles. It's a plan you can mathematically verify. If your plan is given time to work, together with even relatively small contributions, it can grow to a large enterprise. Be an optimist by inclination and a skeptic by training. What to do is simple; carrying it out over twenty years or more is where it becomes difficult. Maybe you just thought to yourself, Twenty years? Is he nuts? I don't have twenty years to work, plan, save, and invest. I might well ask, "Then, what will you be doing? If by process of elimination you aren't doing what is right, aren't you doing what is wrong?"

We, the Jury . . .

The story of *Good Debt, Bad Debt* is really one of stewardship and temperance. The best thing we can pass on to our children is a habit of prudent stewardship and financial temperance. By *stewardship,* I mean careful forethought and planning. By *temperance* I mean the right use of the right things at the right times.

In the preceding I have presented a case for the importance of understanding the debt effects, control of emotions, burn rate, and delayed gratification. You now are the jury foreperson; convene a jury of your friends, especially your financially fit friends, to discuss them. You then render the verdict.

The concept of *Good Debt, Bad Debt* is that not all debt is necessarily bad, any more than all carbohydrates are bad. I have read a few of the books that preach total abstinence from debt. And that is probably not a bad program for many people. It's certainly better than being besotted with consumer debt. Since we are not talking about teenage sex, I favor a program a bit more liberal than total abstinence!

The idea of taking something historically thought of as bad and calling it good is more than a marketing angle or hook. The proper use of debt can be good. It can be a tool, although no less dangerous than a powerful handgun, and judicious use of debt can build wealth. You would only have to read a few biographies of great men, or consider for a moment the purpose of the stock market, to see the effects of good debt (and, sadly, bad debt). Sure, invest in the stock market if you are educated about it. But if you do invest in the stock market, do so after purging yourself of bad debt or any debt that does not support itself. Looking in *The Wall Street Journal* every day for a good investment while loaded with bad debt is like lusting for salt while dying of thirst. The good investment is getting rid of bad debt.

People are always asking me, "Is there really such a thing as good debt?" A good logician will tell you that the existence of a thing is indisputable proof of its possibility. The key to good or bad debt really is a matter of collateral or security. Warren Buffett has used the "good debt" philosophy for years. He buys below market or does not buy—it is all about value investing, nothing more, nothing less. If what you owe for can easily pay its way by being sold, or hopefully from cash flow it produces, then it is good debt. Whenever debt is used for greed, impatience, or an appearance of wealth, it rarely becomes a blessing. While greed and impatience may get a pass once in a while, debt employed to make us appear to be something we are not is always bad debt, and generally has consequences far above the interest paid.

Success is not fully represented by land, stocks and bonds, or cash. In addition to financial capital, we need to add to our store of intellectual capital and spiritual capital. A great number of books have been and will continue to be written on wealth and success. These are perennial topics, and even though comparatively few people will become rich, there is little secret about how to do it. William Matthews in *Getting On in the World* wrote, "The pith of all the world's wisdom on it [getting money] is condensed into a few proverbs. To work hard, to improve small opportunities, to economize, to avoid debt, are the general rules in which is summed up the hoarded experience of centuries, and the most sagacious writers have added little to them."

> *Looking in* The Wall Street Journal *every day for a "good investment" while loaded with bad debt is like lusting for salt while dying of thirst.*

By implication a book on avoiding debt, or at least avoiding most debt, is about being successful. The less encumbered we are, the more free we become, and freedom is all wealth can really buy. It seems that we sell our brains or brawn in the market, but what we are really selling is part of our humanity—our remaining time on this earth. The reality of the world is that it takes cash to ride the train and drink Coca-Cola.

It has been pure joy to research and write this book. Truly, it has been too much fun to call what I have done work. I am still learning. I have much yet to learn. If you go to the Web site for this book, www.gooddebt.com, you will find discussion guides (jury instructions) and white papers, and you can sign up for my free monthly e-mail newsletter. My contact information is included at the back of this book. Feel free to send your comments or questions. I will try my best to answer all e-mail and letters.

I wish for you not just happiness but complete joy.

Glossary

Good Debt, Bad Debt includes several coined words, some of which are trademarks. Here are a few with explanations of how they came to be.

burn rate™—Your fixed operating cost and any money you spend that does not add to your wealth or net worth. This is the amount of money you "burn" through each month. Part of this is usually necessary expenses, but much of it could be converted to wealth.

Consumerati®—Those who spend without regard to the future, because of a thirst for a consumer lifestyle. People engaged in long-term promiscuous spending. In the simplest terms, spendthrifts. I thought of the word as an offshoot of *illiterati* (those who are illiterate). This is meant to be a class of persons making poor consumer choices. It is not gender-specific.

Debtabetes®—Financial diabetes. Diabetes is the inability of the body to process food because of insufficient insulin. Debtabetes is the inability to break down and eliminate debt because of insufficient cash flow. Cash flow is the financial insulin that breaks down and eliminates debt.

Econowise™—I find this coined word to be self-explanatory. The Econowise are those who seek economy and wisdom.

McSpending—Promiscuous small amounts of spending we don't often account for. The five or ten dollars a day of petty cash leakage we may not consider that can add up to millions over twenty years. It is promiscuous in that we don't feel it is important at the time. It is seen as important only later when the cost is counted.

reality income™—Take your net worth and divide it by the number of years you have worked and this is how much you are working for per year. If you have a net worth of $100,000 and have worked for twenty years, you are working for $5,000 per year. Ouch! The balance went to burn rate.

wealth metrics™—A process to determine wealth, based on Buckminster Fuller's writing. Wealth is the number of days forward you can exist without working.

Recommended Reading

See www.gooddebt.com/resources for the latest updates.

Allen, Robert. *The Challenge.* New York: Simon & Schuster, 1987.
———. *Multiple Streams of Income,* 2nd ed. New York: Wiley, 2004.
Bach, David. *Automatic Millionaire.* New York: Broadway Books, 2003.
Barnum, P. T. *The Art of Money Getting.* Available at www.gooddebt.com/resources.
Buford, Bob. *Halftime: Moving from Success to Significance.* New York: Zondervan, 1997.
Burkett, Larry. *How to Manage Your Money.* Chicago: Moody Press, 1991.
Chatzky, Jean. *You Don't Have to Be Rich.* New York: Portfolio, 2003.
Clark, John. *The Money Is the Gravy.* New York: Warner Books, 2003.
Clason, George. *The Richest Man in Babylon.* New York: Plume, 1937.
Croyle, John. *Bringing Out the Winner in Your Child.* Nashville: Cumberland House, 1996.
Danko, William, and Thomas Stanley. *The Millionaire Next Door.* Atlanta: Longstreet Press, 1996.
Easterbrook, Gregg. *The Progress Paradox.* New York: Random House, 2003.
Goleman, Daniel. *Emotional Intelligence.* New York: Bantam, 1995.
Hansen, Mark Victor, and Robert Allen. *The One Minute Millionaire.* New York: Harmony, 2002.
Helmstetter, Shad. *What to Say When You Talk to Yourself.* New York: MJF Books, 1986.
Hill, Napoleon. *Think and Grow Rich.* Connecticut: Ralston Society, 1937.
Hopkins, Tom. *Mastering the Art of Selling Real Estate.* New York: Portfolio, 2004.
Hunt, Mary. *Debt-Proof Living.* Nashville: Broadman & Holman, 1999.
Keller, Gary, et al. *The Millionaire Real Estate Agent.* New York: McGraw-Hill, 2004.

Kiyosaki, Robert, with Sharon L. Lechter. *Rich Dad Poor Dad: Retire Young, Retire Rich.* New York: Warner Books, 2001.

Kroll, Woodrow. *Proverbs: God's Guide for Life's Choices.* Lincoln, Nebr.: Back to the Bible, 1996.

Lund, Frank. *Stack the Logs.* Bloomington, Ill.: Kahuna Business Group, 2004.

Luskin, Fred. *Forgive for Good.* San Francisco: HarperCollins, 2003.

Manning, Robert. *Credit Card Nation.* New York: Basic Books, 2001.

Marden, Orison. Seventy books from 1896 to 1925, including *Architects of Fate, Success, Ambition,* and *Pushing to the Front.* I consider Marden my posthumous mentor. For more on Marden: www.jonhanson.com/marden.

Miller, Jack. *Confessions of a Real Estate Wheeler Dealer.* See: www.cashflow-concepts.com.

Napier, Jimmy. *Invest in Debt.* Chipley, Fla.: Jim Napier, 1983.

Ramsey, Dave. *Financial Peace Revisited.* New York: Viking, 2002.

Rice, Patrick, and Jennifer Dirks. *IRA Wealth.* New York: Square One, 2003.

Rohn, Jim. *Seven Strategies for Wealth and Happiness.* Rocklin, Calif.: Prima Lifestyles, 1996.

Schur, Juliet. *The Overspent American.* New York: Basic Books, 1998.

Scott, Steven. *Mentored by a Millionaire.* New York: Wiley, 2004.

Seligman, Martin. *Authentic Happiness.* New York: Free Press, 2002.

Silverstein, Michael, and Neil Fiske. *Trading Up: The New American Luxury.* New York: Portfolio, 2003.

Smiles, Samuel. *Thrift.* London: Bedford Clark, 1861. See also Smiles's *Character* and *Self-Help.*

Sowell, Thomas. *Inside American Education.* New York: Free Press, 1992.

Stanley, Thomas. *The Millionaire Mind.* New York: Andrews McMeel, 2001.

Taylor, Henry. *Notes from Life: Six Essays. Money, Humility and Independence, Wisdom, Choice in Marriage, Children, The Life Poetic.* London: John Murray, 1848.

Tobias, Cynthia Ulrich. *The Way They Learn.* Colorado Springs: Focus on the Family, 1998.

Tracy, Brian. *Focal Point.* New York: Amacon, 2002.

Waitley, Denis. *The Psychology of Winning,* reissue edition. New York: Berkley, 1992.

Warren, Rick. *The Purpose-Driven Life.* New York: Zondervan, 2002.

Zick, Barney. *The Negotiating Paradox.* Kennett, Mo.: Skyward, 1999.

Ziglar, Zig. *See You at the Top.* Gretna, La.: Pelican, 1985.

Recommended Seminars and Home Study Courses

Brian Tracy International—Personal, business, and professional development; author of the Psychology of Achievement course
www.briantracy.com

Crown Financial Ministries—Budgeting and financial planning; *Money Matters* radio program (48 states)
www.crown.org

Jack Miller—Advanced seminars, real estate and estate planning, cash flow, notes and mortgages, options
www.cashflowconcepts.com

Jim Rohn International—Personal development and leadership
www.jimrohn.com

Jon Hanson Seminars—Topics: cars, houses, spouses; developing your philosophy of debt; *Good Debt, Bad Debt* series
www.gooddebt.com

Mark Victor Hansen—Cocreator of the *Chicken Soup for the Soul* series; personal development, speaking, and publishing materials and seminars
www.markvictorhansen.com

Index

Contact Publisher:
Portfolio
Penguin Group (USA) Inc.
375 Hudson Street
New York, NY 10014
Bulk and Special Sales:
    212-366-2612
www.penguin.com

Contact Author:
Jon Hanson
2965 Taylor Road, #204
Reynoldsburg, OH 43068
jon@gooddebt.com
www.gooddebt.com
www.jonhanson.com

Company- or group-based seminars are available in conjunction with bulk purchases or minimum number of book sales guarantees to be negotiated with the author. Seminars are based on the book and derivative information on the topic of personal finance.

Seminars and presentations are designed in modules and may be customized for a particular company. Speaking fees are sometimes waived depending on the amount of books purchased from a specified source. Contact the author for details.

A full-day seminar covers the topic areas of *Good Debt, Bad Debt.*

A one- or two-hour seminar module is available on most chapter topics.

Jon Hanson may be available as a keynote speaker or presenter for your event.

POPULAR TOPICS:

- Marriage and Money: You Married Who?
- Understanding Burn Rate and Delayed Gratification
- Houses, Spouses, and Cars—Oh My!
- What If You Live? Designing an End Game for Secure Retirement
- Trade Up Mortgage Down Seminar: Real Estate
- The Invisible Hand of Debt: How Debt Takes More Than Just Your Money

The permanent Web site for all updates and discussion guides is www.gooddebt.com.